ROUTLEDGE LIBRARY EDITIONS:
ETHICS

I0028192

Volume 9

THE ETHICS OF SUICIDE

THE ETHICS OF SUICIDE

VICTOR COSCULLUELA

Routledge
Taylor & Francis Group

LONDON AND NEW YORK

First published in 1995 by Garland Publishing Inc.

This edition first published in 2021
by Routledge
2 Park Square, Milton Park, Abingdon, Oxon OX14 4RN

and by Routledge
52 Vanderbilt Avenue, New York, NY 10017

Routledge is an imprint of the Taylor & Francis Group, an informa business

© 1995 Victor Cosculluela

British Library Cataloguing in Publication Data
A catalogue record for this book is available from the British Library

ISBN: 978-0-367-85624-3 (Set)
ISBN: 978-1-00-305260-9 (Set) (ebk)
ISBN: 978-0-367-46249-9 (Volume 9) (hbk)
ISBN: 978-1-00-302775-1 (Volume 9) (ebk)

Publisher's Note
The publisher has gone to great lengths to ensure the quality of this reprint but points out that some imperfections in the original copies may be apparent.

Disclaimer
The publisher has made every effort to trace copyright holders and would welcome correspondence from those they have been unable to trace.

THE ETHICS OF SUICIDE

Victor Cosculluela

GARLAND PUBLISHING, Inc.
New York & London / 1995

Library of Congress Cataloging-in-Publication Data

Cosculluela, Victor.
    The ethics of suicide / by Victor Cosculluela.
        p.   cm. — (Garland studies in applied ethics ;
    vol. 4) (Garland reference library of social science ;
    vol. 1033)
    Includes bibliographical references (p.   )
    and index.
    ISBN 0-8153-2031-0 (acid-free paper)
    1. Suicide—Moral and ethical aspects.   I. Title.
    II. Series: Garland studies in applied ethics ; v. 4.
    III. Series: Garland reference library of social science ;
    v. 1033.
    HV6545.C67   1995
    179'.7—dc20   94-45150
                                                         CIP

Printed on acid-free, 250-year-life paper
Manufactured in the United States of America

For Beatriz

CONTENTS

PREFACE

Suicide raises several ethical questions. Is suicide ever morally permissible? If so, under what kinds of conditions? Is suicide ever morally obligatory? Do the requirements of morality ever demand so much from an individual? Are suicide prevention measures morally justifiable? If so, under what kinds of circumstances? Does morality require us to try to prevent potential suicides from carrying out their intention even if doing so involves coercion? Are we ever permitted, or even obliged, to facilitate suicide?

Suicide also raises an analytical problem. There is a raging controversy concerning the precise meaning of the term "suicide." What are the conditions which an action must meet in order to be classed as suicide?

The following work addresses these and other questions. It defends the claim that suicide is not always morally wrong. In fact, suicide can be obligatory. Further, it is sometimes wrong to prevent someone from killing himself. On the contrary, sometimes one might even be obliged to assist someone who is attempting suicide. Further, a suicide facilitation policy is desirable.

In arguing for these claims, we run up against strong prejudices against all suicide, prejudices which are fueled by anti-suicide arguments which are often uncritically--and even unconsciously--accepted. Therefore, the first two chapters attempt to dispose of many of these arguments. Chapter 1 addresses what I call popular and religious arguments, while chapter 2 addresses what I call philosophical arguments against suicide. Some of the popular and religious arguments addressed in chapter 1 would not merit consideration were it not for the fact that they have been served up again and again in the history of the suicide debate, and, more importantly, they continue to be relied upon today. There is, of course, no hard and fast distinction between popular and religious arguments on the one hand and philosophical arguments on the other. This is simply a convenient way of distinguishing between arguments which differ in importance, the philosophical arguments being the more important variety.

In the ethical portions of this book, I will frequently argue by appealing to common-sense convictions about the moral status of certain acts. For instance, I might assume that readers share my convictions about the conditions under which emigration is morally acceptable. Although the method of appealing to common-sense moral convictions is common in applied ethics, it is hardly infallible. After all, there is no guarantee that the ethical convictions from which reasoning must begin are true. However, if we are going to reason at all about the moral status of suicide--or about the moral status of any act--we have to assume, at least tentatively, that some of the ethical convictions we already have are correct. This is not peculiar to applied ethics since all reasoning must start from assumptions. Admittedly, however, there is greater skepticism about the truth of our common-sense ethical convictions. While I will not attempt a general defense of common-sense ethical convictions--how *could* one defend common-sense ethical convictions without appealing to those very convictions?--I try to appeal to moral beliefs that my readers presumably share.

After addressing anti-suicide arguments in chapters 1 and 2, and after treating permissible and obligatory suicide in chapter 3, and the prevention and facilitation issues in chapter 4, I consider the views of Schopenhauer and Camus on suicide in chapter 5. Both argue that the ideal person will refrain from suicide, even though suicide may be morally permissible. Although their views are certainly interesting and important, they are quite complex, and because neither argues that suicide is impermissible, their views are discussed after the main ethical debates in suicide are considered.

In the appendix, a definition of "suicide" will be defended. However, it will also be argued that the attempt to give a precise definition of "suicide" which will be acceptable to all reflective people is based on some naive assumptions. Nevertheless, I defend a definition of suicide which seems to me to accurately reflect what most people regard as the essence of suicide.

Since notes usually distract readers, those in this book never add important points to the text; at most they add trivial material, and even this occurs only rarely. Consequently, all notes can be safely ignored by readers who are uninterested in bibliographic details or minor points.

ACKNOWLEDGMENTS

Without the encouragement and advice of Professor Alan Goldman of the University of Miami, who read several versions of this work, the present book would have been even more imperfect than it is. His influence on the quality of this book was, in my opinion, wholly positive, and his willingness to sacrifice his time and energy on my behalf was truly remarkable. Of course, I alone am responsible for the remaining errors, some of which undoubtedly arise from my occasional unwillingness to follow his advice.

I would also like to thank my wife Beatriz for her unfailing encouragement.

Finally, I thank *The International Journal of Applied Philosophy* for allowing me to reproduce previously published material on suicide prevention.

CHAPTER 1

POPULAR AND RELIGIOUS ARGUMENTS AGAINST SUICIDE

In this chapter we will consider various popular and religious arguments for the claim that suicide is morally wrong. By a "popular argument," I mean an argument that would very likely be employed by the average person without philosophical training. By a "religious argument," I mean an argument that is expressed in the context of religious beliefs, such as the belief that God exists. As we shall see, however, some religious arguments against suicide can be reinterpreted in a non-religious way. Religious arguments are treated together with popular arguments since there is obviously a great deal of overlap between the two categories thanks to the widespread acceptance of religious claims.

Some of the arguments we will discuss would not merit consideration were it not for the fact that they have been served up again and again in the history of the debate on the ethics of suicide. Further, they continue to influence the thinking of contemporary authors. One sometimes finds these arguments offered as conclusive reasons for condemning suicide. For these and other reasons, it would be inappropriate to ignore them entirely.

Is Suicide Unnatural?

Suicide is often condemned on the ground that it is "unnatural" in some sense. The suicide does not follow "nature's way."[1] Since different arguments can be expressed by the claim that suicide is unnatural, we must consider various possible formulations.

Suicide and the will to live: On one interpretation, both St. Thomas Aquinas and Josephus argued that suicide is unnatural in

3

the sense that it is a violation of the alleged ever-present drive which all living organisms have to preserve their lives. According to Aquinas, since "everything naturally keeps itself in being, and resists corruption as far as it can," it follows that "suicide is contrary to the inclination of nature." From this he inferred that "suicide is always a mortal sin."[2] Likewise, Josephus claimed that suicide is "repugnant to that nature which all creatures share" since among the animals "there is not one that deliberately seeks death or kills itself; so firmly rooted is all nature's law--the will to live."[3]

Before we consider this argument, it is important to note that despite the phrase "suicide is always a mortal sin" in the quotation from Aquinas, he does not condemn suicide in all possible circumstances. For Aquinas, every case of suicide is morally wrong except for the extremely rare cases in which God Himself directly commands the act.[4] In what follows I will generally ignore this qualification since I will not be concerned with suicides which are directly commanded by God Himself.

On one interpretation of Aquinas[5] and Josephus, their argument is that suicide is morally wrong because it involves a failure to follow the alleged innate and ever-present drive which every living organism has to preserve its life. Let us call this drive the "life drive." Their argument, on this interpretation, may be formulated as follows:

(1)   Every living organism has a life drive.

(2)   If every living organism has a life drive, then every case of suicide involves a violation of the suicide's life drive.

(3)   If every case of suicide involves a violation of the suicide's life drive, then suicide is never morally permissible.

(4)   Therefore, suicide is never morally permissible.

I am willing to grant premise (2) for the sake of argument.[6] So my evaluation will focus on (1) and (3). Of these two premises, (3) is the more dubious.

According to (1), every living organism has an innate and ever-present drive to preserve its life. This claim raises several problems. First, as several authors have noted, there is evidence that self-destructive behavior is not unknown even among non-human animals. Some evidence suggests that self-destructive behavior is genetically selected for when the death of an individual organism creates for related members of the same species advantages which outweigh the genetic value of its own survival.[7] Self-destruction has been observed in dogs, who may kill themselves by drowning themselves or by refusing food, for various reasons.[8] Second, the mere fact that human beings commit suicide may weaken the claim that every organism has an ever-present drive to preserve its life. It is arguable that many human beings have no desire whatsoever to preserve their lives.

However, the proponent of (1) is in a position to admit that non-human animals perform acts of self-destruction, and that human beings commit suicide--of course they do--while claiming that these facts are compatible with (1), since it is possible that when these events occur, the life drive is not absent but overpowered by some other drive, say, a drive to escape pain. The idea here is that from the mere fact that an organism performs a certain act (e.g., suicide), it does not follow that it had no desire at all to refrain from performing that act. It has been suggested that suicidal persons would prefer to go on living but are willing to do so only if their prospects were less bleak.[9] Perhaps, then, when non-human animals perform self-destructive acts and when human beings commit suicide, what happens is that their life drive is not their strongest source of motivation. This objection does show that the evidence concerning self-destructive behavior in non-human animals and suicide in human beings is not conclusive against (1). However, what this evidence does show is that (1) is not in any way obvious or self-evident. While it may be obvious that animals usually strive to preserve their lives, it is not at all obvious that they have an *ever-present* drive to do so. Thus, (1) is not obviously true, and its truth is not established by pointing out the evolutionary value of a general tendency in animals to preserve their lives; as pointed out above, evolutionary theory itself may conflict with (1).

However, it will be safer for us to assume that (1) is true. The present argument against suicide would still fail if (3) were shown to be false. (3) claims that if every case of suicide involves a failure to follow the suicide's life drive, then suicide is never morally permissible. This claim seems implausible. Why should the fact--assuming it is a fact--that suicide conflicts with a certain drive have any bearing on the moral status of the act? Aquinas and Josephus may be assuming the principle that if an act conflicts with a "natural" (i.e., innate) drive, that act is morally wrong.[10] Given this principle, (3) can be defended. But this principle is itself totally implausible. As John Donne suggested in *Biathanatos*, the first work published in English (1647) to challenge the traditional Christian condemnation of suicide, if the fact that an act conflicts with a natural drive is sufficient to make it morally wrong, then celibacy would be morally wrong since it violates the natural desire for sexual gratification.[11] Likewise, donating to charities, monogamy, honesty, and other practices which we praise are frequently contrary to our natural inclinations, but surely this fact alone does not establish that those practices are wrong. So the principle that any act which is contrary to a natural drive is thereby morally wrong is implausible. Consequently, (3) cannot be rescued by this principle. Further, in the absence of this principle, (3) seems implausible. From the mere fact that a case of suicide violates the suicide's life drive it cannot be inferred that it is morally wrong. Likewise, even if a case of martyrdom conflicted with the martyr's life drive, that in itself would not render the act wrong.

Suicide and prescriptive natural law: Some philosophers have claimed that while the above interpretation may apply to Josephus, it does not apply to Aquinas. Consequently, they claim that the objection just rehearsed (i.e., that some acts which are contrary to our inclinations are morally right) is irrelevant to Aquinas's argument. Tom Beauchamp clearly expressed this position:

> This interpretation overlooks the fact that Thomistic philosophers draw an important distinction between laws of nature and natural laws. Presumably, the former are descriptive statements . . . while the latter are prescriptive statements derived from philosophical knowledge of the essential properties of human nature. . . . In this theory, natural laws do not empirically *describe* behavior. . . ; rather, they delimit the behavior that is morally appropriate for a human being; they tell us how we *ought* to behave because of our very nature as humans.[12]

On this view, there is a "natural law" that applies to human beings. This natural law is, as Margaret Battin notes, a prescriptive principle which requires human beings to "live and to engage in specifically human activities" that "promote the fulfillment of man's highest potential. Suicide is wrong because it precludes these activities."[13] So when Aquinas classes suicide as an act which is contrary to "natural law," what he means is that the act is contrary to a prescriptive principle which applies to human beings because of their potentialities as human beings. As Frederick Copleston, a contemporary Thomist, puts it, the natural law is "the totality of the universal precepts or dictates" regarding "the good which is to be pursued and the evil which is to be shunned"; "man has a natural tendency to preserve his being, and reason reflecting on this tendency as present in man promulgates the precept that life is to be preserved."[14] Aquinas's own words put this interpretation beyond dispute:

> . . . this is the first precept of [the natural] law, that *good is to be done and promoted, and evil is to be avoided*. All other precepts of the natural law are based upon this. . . .[15]

With respect to the present issue he says that whatever is a means of preserving life "belongs to the natural law."[16]

With this in mind, we can consider Beauchamp's formulation of the Thomistic argument:

(i)   It is a natural law that everything loves and seeks to perpetuate itself.

(ii)   Suicide is an act contrary to self-love and self-perpetuation.

(iii)   (Therefore) suicide is contrary to natural law.

(iv)   Anything contrary to natural law is morally wrong.

(v)   (Therefore) suicide is morally wrong.[17]

Although Beauchamp himself criticizes this argument on the ground that the Thomistic distinction between laws of nature and natural laws is "far too obscure to be convincing,"[18] I will not pursue this kind of criticism. Instead, I will consider first premise (ii) and then premise (i).

Premise (ii) asserts that suicide is contrary to self-love and self-perpetuation. Clearly, suicide is contrary to self-perpetuation since we are concerned here with bodily self-perpetuation (i.e., perpetuation as a living embodied being). However, it is unclear that suicide is contrary to self-love. One can, it seems, commit suicide without abandoning self-love; for instance, one can commit suicide in order to spare oneself a great deal of suffering. Out of self-love, one can put an end to one's life in order to free oneself from pain.

However, it is open to the Thomist to simply rewrite (ii) as follows:

(ii')   Suicide is an act contrary to self-perpetuation.

Having rewritten (ii) as (ii'), the reference to self-love in premise (i) is no longer an essential part of the argument; it does no logical work since self-love is not referred to in premise (ii'). So (i) can be rewritten as follows:

(i')   It is a natural law that everything seeks to perpetuate itself.

Given the prescriptive meaning of "natural law," (i') is not a purely descriptive statement. Since to say that there is a "natural law" requiring the performance of an act is to say that the act is obligatory, (i') must be saying that *it is obligatory for every living thing to seek to perpetuate itself*. It should now be clear that, without further argument, our revised Thomistic argument simply assumes that suicide is wrong; that is, premise (i') begs the question. Once we interpret "natural law" in a prescriptive sense, we cannot simply assume from the start that seeking self-perpetuation is required by the natural law. To do so is simply to assume from the start that suicide is morally wrong. So it seems that even under the new interpretation of Aquinas, his argument fails to establish the immorality of suicide, unless some independent reason can be found for accepting (i'). In the next section we will examine possible independent grounds for accepting (i'); since Aquinas believed that the natural law derives from God's "eternal law,"[19] perhaps the present argument can be revived.

Suicide and God's control of life and death: When giving what I will later call the "Divine Gift Argument," which makes the familiar claim that life is a gift from God, Aquinas condemned suicide on the ground that "it belongs to God alone to pronounce sentence of death and life."[20] On one interpretation, this asserts that suicide is unnatural in that it meddles with God's preferred schedule of human death. That is, God wants people to die at certain times and in certain ways, and to commit suicide is to meddle with His divine wishes. Let us call these wishes "God's death wishes for human beings." This version of the argument can be formulated as follows:

(A)   All suicide frustrates God's death wishes for human beings.

(B)   All acts which frustrate God's death wishes for human beings are morally wrong.

(C)   Therefore, all suicide is morally wrong.

Unlike other religious arguments which we will consider, this argument cannot be divorced from its theological assumptions. So at least one obvious difficulty facing this argument is that, from a purely philosophical standpoint, it assumes something extremely controversial: God's existence.

Premise (A) is the main weak point of this argument. It claims that all suicide frustrates God's death wishes for human beings. How could this possibly be established? Perhaps the defender of this argument will appeal to the Bible. However, this can hardly be compelling from a purely philosophical standpoint, and millions of theists are themselves willing to abandon many of the Bible's claims. (See the discussion below of the Biblical case against suicide.) Perhaps (A) could be known by means of a special communication from God. But that such a communication has taken place has not been established. It seems, then, that the only way to establish (A) is to show that all suicide is morally wrong; having shown that, one could claim that since God never wishes us to perform morally wrong acts, suicide always frustrates God's wishes. Of course, this move simply starts from the assumption that all suicide is wrong. Thus, even if we grant God's existence, this argument still faces serious problems.

However, there is another way to interpret Aquinas's argument. He claimed that

> life . . . is subject to His power, Who kills and makes to live. Hence, whoever takes his own life, sins against God. . . . For it belongs to God alone to pronounce sentence of death and life, according to Deut. xxxii 39, *I will kill and I will make to live.*[21]

The phrase "it belongs to God alone" suggests that God alone is permitted to kill human beings. To commit suicide is to take matters into one's own hands. Suicide is "unnatural" in this sense. It not only frustrates God's wishes, it meddles with his divine role; with respect to death, "the time is reserved for God alone," as a contemporary proponent of this argument put it.[22]

The argument here cannot be that God alone kills human beings since if God alone killed human beings, then all killing would be God's work; as such, God would not find fault with any killing whatsoever, even the mass exterminations carried out by the Nazi and Soviet regimes. So what the argument seems to be saying is that God alone has the right to kill human beings. And the passage from Aquinas suggests a reason for this: God's position relative to human beings is that of judge; only He can "pronounce sentence." So the argument seems to be that, since only God has the right to deliver a death sentence, all suicide is wrong.

Aside from the fact that this argument cannot be divorced from its theological assumptions, it faces at least two other difficulties. First, capital punishment is a controversial topic; those who think that capital punishment is wrong might make the extreme claim that no being ever has the right to deliver a death sentence, not even God (if He exists). On the other hand, proponents of capital punishment might claim that earthly judges also have the right to deliver a death sentence. So the claim that only God has the right to deliver a death sentence should not seem obvious, even for theists. A second and more basic problem is that this argument assumes that to commit suicide is to inflict the death penalty on oneself. But there are many possible motives for suicide; for example, the motive may be to spare oneself apparently pointless suffering. Suicide as self-inflicted capital punishment is hardly the standard case.

Suicide and normality: Perhaps when suicide is condemned in popular circles on the ground that it is unnatural, what is meant is that suicide is abnormal in the sense that it is not an act performed by the vast majority; most people die a "natural death."

But from the fact that an act is abnormal in the sense that only a small minority of people performs that act, it clearly does not follow that it is morally wrong. From the fact that relatively few people obey a certain traffic law, it does not follow that obeying that law is morally wrong. Again, from the mere fact that relatively few people engage in lifelong celibacy it does not follow that lifelong celibacy is morally wrong. If most people committed rape, surely that would not make refraining from rape morally wrong. Thus, if the claim that suicide is unnatural means merely that it is abnormal in the specified sense, this argument fails to show that suicide is morally wrong.

Suicide and mental illness: A related argument might claim not merely that the vast majority of people refrains from the act, but that suicide is a product of mental illness. Since every case of suicide must be the product of mental illness, every case of suicide must be morally wrong.

The psychological claim in this argument would be very difficult to establish since a suicide's mental status at the time of the act is seldom known.[23] Nevertheless, some social scientists claim that suicide is very frequently committed by people suffering from some form of mental disturbance (e.g., depression), even though not all cases of suicide result from mental illness.[24] Further, after a careful review of the recent findings on the question "Is the person who attempts or commits suicide mentally ill?," Battin concludes that the empirical evidence clearly points to the conclusion that suicide is not necessarily connected with mental illness.[25] Even if many suicides are associated with some form of mental illness, not all are. More importantly, even if many cases of suicide are associated with mental illness, it clearly does not follow that it is impossible for a psychologically healthy individual to commit suicide. The latter claim has been explicitly denied even within the social sciences, where it has been conceded that "a psychologically healthy person, faced with the certainty of being tortured to death, might commit suicide."[26] I conclude that even if most actual cases of suicide are associated with some form of mental illness (e.g., chronic depression), it is false that all actual cases are so associated, and it is clearly false all psychologically possible cases of suicide are associated with mental illness. (More will be said about the relation between mental illness and suicide in Chapter 4.)

However, even if we admit the assumption that suicide is always a product of mental illness, it does not follow that suicide is always morally impermissible. Even if every case of suicide were associated with mental illness, that would do nothing to establish the general immorality of suicide. Suppose it could be shown that it is psychologically impossible for someone to engage in voluntary lifelong celibacy without suffering from some mental abnormality such as a neurosis. It would then be psychologically impossible for a mentally healthy person to engage in voluntary lifelong celibacy. However, it would not follow from this finding that voluntary lifelong celibacy is morally impermissible. Likewise, even if having a sudden stroke of musical genius turned out to be associated with some form of neurosis, that fact alone would not establish the immorality of having strokes of musical genius. The same holds for suicide. Even if it were a fact that suicide is necessarily associated with some form of mental disturbance, nothing at all would follow concerning the moral status of suicide.

Suicide and the Bible

Some people see no need to look beyond the Bible for an argument against suicide; suicide, they say, is wrong since the Bible condemns the act. Unfortunately for this argument, there is very widespread agreement that the Bible nowhere explicitly condemns suicide.[27] One important passage, of course, is the commandment against killing. St. Augustine claimed that the commandment "Thou shalt not kill" (Exodus 20:13) can be taken to imply that "suicide is a detestable and damnable wickedness"[28] (unless the act is commanded by God either directly or through a "just law"). However, even this claim has been denied. For example, it has been claimed that the commandment is best translated "Thou shalt do no wrongful killing." It is then pointed out that nowhere in the Old Testament does the phrase "wrongful killing" appear in relation to suicide. Nor is there any philological reason to believe that suicide falls under this phrase. Thus, the commandment "Thou shalt do no wrongful killing" is insufficient for a general condemnation of suicide, since suicide may not always count as "wrongful killing"; that suicide is an instance of wrongful killing would have to be independently shown.[29]

However, Darrel Amundsen, who admits that the Bible does not explicitly condemn suicide, has recently argued at length that

> the New Testament encourages patience, stresses hope, commands perseverance, and so strongly emphasizes the sovereignty of God in the life of Christians and the trust that they should exercise, knowing that God will cause all things to work out for their good, that it is unlikely that suicide to escape from those very trials which God had chosen to inflict or permit could be regarded as anything less than a breach of trust.[30]

For Amundsen, although the Bible nowhere explicitly condemns suicide, it is permeated by a moral viewpoint which is generally inimical to suicide.

Of course, we can simply grant that suicide is opposed to the spirit of the Bible since, from a purely philosophical standpoint, whether or not the Bible condemns suicide (implicitly or explicitly) is wholly irrelevant. It is surprising to find that some contemporary philosophers feel obliged to dispute the correct interpretation of various Biblical passages. Even if the Bible consistently and repeatedly condemned suicide in the most explicit language, this would be irrelevant from a purely philosophical standpoint (although, of course, it would not be irrelevant from other standpoints). For the Bible's word to count as philosophically authoritative, it would first have to be shown that God exists and that the Bible is genuinely the word of God, or at least that the Bible has been a perfectly reliable source of truth in the past. The claim that we have shown any of these things is, of course, extremely controversial, and for this reason the argument which condemns suicide on Biblical grounds is entirely worthless.

It is also interesting to note that other claims made in the Bible are dismissed by millions of Christians. For example, homosexual practices between men are condemned in the Bible in no uncertain terms (Leviticus 18:22); the Bible seems to suggest that men who engage in homosexual practices should be killed (Leviticus 20:13). Yet millions of Christians would find the latter position morally unacceptable. The Bible also explicitly gives human beings freedom to eat animals (Genesis 9:2-3). Nevertheless, many Christians oppose the eating of meat on moral grounds. The Bible even declares that anyone with a contagious skin disease must wear torn clothing and disordered hair and repeatedly shout that he is unclean (Leviticus 13:45-46). Luckily, few if any of the millions of Christians feel obliged to follow this rule. The Bible declares that every man who divorces his wife and marries another is thereby guilty of adultery, and that every man who marries a divorced woman is likewise guilty of adultery (Luke 16:18; Matthew 5:32; 19:9). Here again millions of Christians feel that divorce is morally permissible in various kinds of cases. In short, then, there are many passages in both the Old and New Testaments which would seem to millions of Christians to embody morally unacceptable (if not repulsive) viewpoints. In such cases, these Christians ignore the Bible's pronouncements. So even if the Bible condemned all suicide in the most explicit terms, that in itself should not suffice to convince these same millions of Christians that suicide is morally wrong in all cases. One cannot arbitrarily select some passages of the Bible (i.e., those one happens to find appealing) as correctly reflecting the attitude of the deity while dismissing others (i.e., those one finds absurd) as mere products of human folly.

Analogy-Based Religious Arguments[31]

We now turn to a set of religious arguments which rely on analogies to describe the relationship between human beings and God. On the basis of these analogies, it is argued that suicide is always, or virtually always, wrong. For example, Josephus employed what I will call the Divine Gift Argument: since our existence is a gift from God, "He is indignant when man treats His gift with scorn."[32] Aquinas repeated this familiar theme: since "life is God's gift to man," "whoever takes his own life, sins against God."[33]

Plato put forward the similar Divine Possession Argument, which relies on the assumption that human beings are owned by the gods,[34] while Locke appealed to the closely related Divine Handiwork Argument: since people are "all the workmanship of one omnipotent and infinitely wise Maker," it follows that they are "made to last during His, not another's pleasure."[35]

Locke also employed the frequently repeated Divine Post Argument: since people are "the servants of one sovereign Master, sent into the world by His order and about His business," everyone is "bound to preserve himself, and not to quit his station willfully."[36]

Josephus also delivered the Divine Deposit Argument, according to which the soul "is a portion of the Deity housed in our bodies." If "one who makes away with or misapplies a deposit entrusted to him by a fellow-man is reckoned a perjured villain," asked Josephus, "how can he who casts out from his body the deposit which God has placed there, hope to elude Him whom he has thus wronged?"[37]

These are some of the most well-known analogy-based religious arguments that have been offered against suicide. They are repeated again and again in classical discussions of suicide, as if their constant repetition ensured their soundness. Even Kant found it necessary to resort to analogy-based religious arguments; the suicide, he claimed, "arrives in the other world as someone who has deserted his post"; in fact, he arrives there "as a rebel against God." Further, "God is our owner; we are His property."[38]

It should be noted that those who use these arguments are not thereby committed to the position that suicide is wrong *because* God forbids it. Kant was clear that "suicide is not inadmissible and abominable because God has forbidden it; God has forbidden it because it is abominable."[39] So we cannot criticize proponents of analogy-based religious arguments on the ground that such arguments presuppose a "divine command" theory of ethics, according to which the moral status of an act is a function of God's commands; an act is morally obligatory because God happens to command it, while an act is morally wrong because God happens to forbid it.

Of course, the major problem facing all analogy-based religious arguments without exception is that such arguments assume that God (or at least a god) exists. All proponents of such arguments must accept this assumption. So even if the analogy-based religious arguments were otherwise sound, they would carry little philosophical weight since they all depend on an assumption which is controversial in the extreme.

However, we may briefly note a few other objections. Consider first the Divine Gift Argument. We are told that because life is God's gift to human beings it would be wrong to destroy this gift by means of suicide. The idea here is that we owe God some sort of gratitude for His gift of life, and suicide is incompatible with such gratitude.[40] On the contrary, as one contemporary proponent of this argument put it, suicide is "an insult to the very gift of life itself."[41]

However, as Hume pointed out, it is possible for a suicide to feel gratitude both for the gift of life and the gift of being able to end it when circumstances become unbearable: "But I thank providence, both for the good which I have already enjoyed, and for the power with which I am endowed of escaping the ill that threatens me."[42] He quotes with approval Seneca's pronouncement: "And let us thank God that no man can be kept in life."[43] The attitude of someone who is contemplating suicide might be one of deep gratitude to God for the gift of life combined with deep gratitude for the gift of being able to find relief through suicide. This attitude is illustrated in the following passage from an actual suicide note:

> We have both had very full and satisfying lives.
> Pitney [the husband] has worked very hard and with
> great dedication for the church. I have had an
> adventurous and happy life. We both had happy lives
> and our children have crowned this happiness. . . .[44]

Of course, the proponent of the Divine Gift Argument might insist that suicide is incompatible with full or absolute gratitude to God for the gift of life; the person who employs the alleged gift of suicide, it might be said, may feel some high degree of gratitude to God, but she cannot feel absolute or full gratitude. But this reply is *ad hoc*; there seems to be no good reason for insisting that because someone has destroyed a gift, it thereby follows that he did not fully appreciate it. Consider a soldier who has been captured by ruthless enemies who are going to give him a drug which will cause him to reveal military secrets. The soldier may commit suicide in order to avoid revealing information which would be used to kill thousands of his comrades. Is it really impossible for this soldier to feel full gratitude for the gift of life? It seems clear that he might feel full gratitude to God for the gift of life and yet also feel gratitude for the opportunity to spare his comrades an agonizing annihilation. It seems, then, that suicide is not incompatible with full gratitude to God for the gift of life.

The Divine Possession Argument appeals to the claim that human beings are God's property (perhaps his slaves). As Kant stated in the passage quoted above, "God is our owner; we are His property." Likewise, in 1958 Pope Pius XII condemned suicide on the ground that "Life belongs to God."[45] But, on the assumption that God exists and is somehow responsible for the existence of everything else, *everything* God creates would appear to be his property; trees and rivers would also count as God's possessions. The reason why human beings are God's possessions is also the reason why trees and rivers are God's possessions. Yet there are numerous occasions on which there is nothing morally wrong with destroying a particular tree or river. If a tree is growing in such a way that it will destroy an orphanage unless it is destroyed, it is morally permissible to destroy it. The reply from the proponent of the Divine Possession Argument will be that God has given us permission to tamper with his other possessions, but He has not given us permission to tamper with His highest possessions, human beings, by means of suicide. This is possible; however, to establish the claim that God has not given us permission to commit suicide in certain situations, an argument other than the Divine Possession Argument must be employed. The reason is that from the fact that something is one of God's possessions it does not follow that it is always morally wrong to tamper with or destroy it. So the Divine Possession Argument will have to rely on some other argument.

The difficulty which faces the Divine Possession Argument also faces the related Divine Handiwork Argument. From the fact that something (e.g., a certain tree) is God's handiwork, it does not follow that it is morally wrong for human beings to tamper with or even kill it. To show that it is always wrong to tamper with God's highest handiworks by means of suicide, some other argument must be given; merely saying that human beings are made by God is not sufficient.

Proponents of the Divine Possession Argument and the Divine Handiwork Argument would most likely turn to the Divine Post Argument. This argument claims that because God has given each person a task to perform, it is immoral to commit suicide; the suicide "has deserted his post," as Kant put it in a passage quoted earlier.

This is perhaps the best of the analogy-based religious arguments. However, one problem is that it is very difficult to know one's post in life. For all that has been said so far, one's post in life might involve suicide. Perhaps one has been given the task of committing suicide in order to set an example for others who are suffering from agonizing mental or physical pain. Another problem with this argument is that, for all it claims, it is possible that God Himself releases us from our posts and permits us to commit suicide in certain situations. Consider the following passages from Montaigne and Hume respectively:

> God gives us leave enough to go when He is pleased to reduce us to such a condition that to live is far worse than to die.[46]

> . . . whenever pain or sorrow so far overcome my patience, as to make me tired of life, I may conclude that I am recalled from my station in the clearest and most express terms.[47]

What these passages suggest is that, for all the Divine Post Argument claims, it is possible that the occasions on which people might consider suicide are precisely the occasions on which God allows them to retire from their posts by means of suicide. Some argument other than the Divine Post Argument is necessary to show that this is not the case.

The Divine Deposit Argument seems to merit little attention. Clearly the thesis that each human soul is a "portion" of God is not likely to win wide acceptance. It seems to make little (if any) sense when taken literally. If the claim that each human soul is a portion of God means simply that God has given us life, then the Divine Deposit Argument simply collapses into the Divine Gift Argument. Josephus's remarks (in the passage quoted earlier) suggest that what he had in mind is that souls are loaned to human beings by God and should therefore be returned only when the latter recalls them. The reason why we cannot return our souls early is that God has placed us here so that we can perform a task. On this interpretation, the

Divine Deposit Argument simply reduces to the Divine Post Argument and therefore suffers from the same defects.

Cowardice, Endurance, and Suffering

It is frequently said that suicide is a mark of cowardice. Several philosophers who have made significant contributions to the discussion of suicide have expressed this view. For example, we find Aristotle claiming that to commit suicide to escape painful circumstances "is not the mark of a brave man, but rather of a coward" since "it is softness to fly from what is troublesome, and such a man endures death not because it is noble but to fly from evil."[48] Likewise, Josephus claimed that "there could be no more arrant coward than the pilot who, for fear of a tempest, deliberately sinks his ship before the storm."[49]

A similar argument claims that suicide manifests a lack of patient endurance. This position is usually implied in early Christian sources.[50] For example, Augustine asked,

> Is it not rather proof of a feeble mind, to be unable to bear either the pains of bodily servitude or the foolish opinion of the vulgar? And is not that to be pronounced the greater mind, which rather faces than flees the ills of life. . . ?[51]

Unlike analogy-based religious arguments, this argument can be divorced from its usual religious context, since patient endurance can be treated as a virtue in a non-religious morality. One might then argue that suicide is wrong because it is a manifestation of a lack of patient endurance.

A related thesis asserts the character-building value of suffering. This too is usually expressed in a religious context: "suffering for the Christian should be viewed as something in which he can rejoice" since "God is using the suffering as a means of causing his child to grow spiritually."[52] However, we can divorce the claim that suffering is of value from its usual religious context since it is possible to think of suffering as in some way beneficial to the sufferer without referring to any controversial religious beliefs. Suffering on this view is valuable in the sense that it "builds character," to use a popular expression. The problem with suicide, on this view, is that the suicide avoids the possibility of character development through suffering.

Thus, we must evaluate the following three arguments: suicide is impermissible since it (1) manifests cowardice, (2) manifests a lack of patient endurance, and since (3) in killing himself the suicide thereby forgoes character development through suffering. We can consider these claims in turn.

(1) Several philosophers have claimed that *refraining* from suicide is due to cowardice. Montaigne clearly expressed this view:

> Why dost thou complain of this world? it detains thee not; thy own cowardice is the cause, if thou livest in pain. There needs no more to die than the will to die.[53]

Montaigne's claim is that cowardice is one reason why people suffering from prolonged mental or physical pain refrain from suicide. This suggests the view that all those who commit suicide to save themselves from long-term suffering are manifesting courage. On this view, all cases of avoidance-motivated suicide (i.e., suicide motivated primarily by the desire to avoid personal suffering) manifest courage. The above quotation from Aristotle, on the other hand, suggests the view that all avoidance-motivated suicides are products of cowardice.

The truth seems to be that while some avoidance-motivated suicides manifest cowardice, others do not. Consider the case of a soldier who commits suicide to avoid participation in a battle which he himself knows to be just. Although he knows that the battle is morally justified, he stages his own "accidental" death by "falling" from a high cliff in order to avoid the horrors of combat. There seems to be a great deal of plausibility in the claim that this soldier commits suicide through cowardice. On the other hand, consider a soldier who is fighting courageously in a battle. He is fatally wounded, and he knows that unless he commits suicide his death will be prolonged and agonizing. He does not fear this pain but would prefer not to suffer it. Further, he knows that he is no longer in a position to help his comrades in battle. So he shoots himself.

Here we seem to have a case of avoidance-motivated suicide which is not the result of cowardice.

Consider also the case of a person who commits suicide in public in some extremely shocking way with the intention of thereby making a political or moral statement and the case of a man who commits suicide by arranging his own "accidental" death so that his family can collect insurance money. Here we have two cases of suicide which fall outside the avoidance-motivated class. It seems hopelessly implausible to insist that all such suicides must be manifestations of cowardice. On the contrary, to commit suicide in some excruciatingly painful way in order to make an important political or moral statement requires a great deal of courage. Given our general fear of death and our extreme antipathy toward excruciating pain, someone who willingly brings both upon herself for a cause which she perceives to be noble is manifesting a great deal of courage.

There remains a more basic problem for the present argument against suicide. For the argument to be relevant to the question of whether suicide is ever morally permissible, it would have to claim that *if a given suicide results from cowardice, it is morally impermissible*. This claim rests on the more general claim that *if a particular act results from cowardice, it is morally impermissible*. This latter claim is false, for permissible and even obligatory acts can result from cowardice. To say that an act results from cowardice is to say that it results from a certain motive. But one can perform acts which one is obliged to perform from innumerable motives, not all of which are admirable. For instance, one can save the life of a drowning child simply in order to receive a reward. One has done the right thing from an unpraiseworthy motive. Likewise, one can save the life of a drowning child simply because one is afraid of the public condemnation that one would receive by refusing to save the child. Here, one does the right thing from a cowardly motive. If we knew that a certain person saved a drowning child, we would declare the action morally permissible (or even obligatory). If we later discovered that his action resulted from cowardice, we would no longer praise *him*, but the *action* would still be seen as morally permissible (or obligatory). So, it is false that every act which results from cowardice is morally wrong. If this is right, then no action is morally impermissible simply on the ground that it results from cowardice. One can do the wrong thing from praiseworthy motives, and one can do the right thing from cowardly motives, in which case the agent does not merit praise. Any argument that, like the present argument, condemns a particular act of suicide on the basis of the suicide's motives is unsound since to condemn the motives behind an act is to condemn the agent rather than the act itself. (To say, with Kant, that an act which results from an unpraiseworthy motive has no "moral worth" is not to say that the act is not right, as Kant himself makes clear; actions may be in "accordance with duty" even when they are not "done from duty."[54]) Of course, if someone commits suicide for some morally reprehensible reason, that *person* should be considered morally bad, but his *action* may nevertheless be permissible.

So our reply to the present argument against suicide is that not all suicide results from cowardice. Suicide can even be the result of extreme courage. Further, even if a particular suicide resulted from cowardly motives, that does not determine the rightness or wrongness of the act, though it should affect our estimation of the moral character of the agent.

(2) The second claim we have to consider asserts that suicide is wrong because it manifests a lack of patient endurance. We can admit that patient endurance is a desirable character trait. However, there are limits to the amount of patient endurance which we require of people. For example, if someone accidentally puts his hand into a fire, we do not condemn his quick removal of it on the ground that this act manifests a lack of patient endurance. We might be impressed (or puzzled) by his endurance if he slowly removed his roasting hand from the fire (in which case we might consider him a likely candidate for institutionalization), but we would not condemn quick removal as morally wrong. Likewise, we do not condemn the action of a person undergoing heart surgery who allows a doctor to give him an anesthetic. If such a person refused the anesthetic, we would regard his endurance as quite foolish. What such examples suggest is that we require people to exhibit patient endurance in the face of avoidable suffering only when there is some greater good achieved by their suffering. If their suffering is avoidable and enduring it would not bring about anything good enough to significantly outweigh the negative value of the suffering (as in the cases just rehearsed), we do not require them to endure it.

In many cases in which one might contemplate suicide, these conditions are satisfied. The suffering is avoidable (by means of suicide), and the potential suicide's suffering might not bring about anything good enough so that enduring the suffering is worthwhile. Suppose, for example, that I am alone in a log cabin in the remote wilderness. Suddenly a fire breaks out in the cabin. I am faced with two options. I can either shoot myself in the head with my pistol, or I can allow myself to burn to death. By patiently enduring the pain of burning to death I would achieve nothing of comparable positive value. In this case, I can avoid the pain of burning to death by shooting myself. I am, therefore, not obliged to patiently endure the suffering involved in burning to death.

Another problem with the call for patient endurance arises from the fact that, once again, not all suicides are of the pain-avoidance variety. Suppose that I am not personally suffering from any physical or mental pain, but if I commit suicide in a certain way I can bring about social awareness concerning something horrible the government is doing (e.g., genocide). In such a case, the call for patient endurance is irrelevant, for I myself am not suffering any pain. The concept of patient endurance might then be expanded to cover the pain suffered by others; it might be said that I have to patiently endure the suffering of others at the mercy of an evil government. But patient endurance in the face of grotesque injustice which I could reduce by abandoning patient endurance hardly seems obligatory, and in general patient endurance of the suffering of others hardly seems praiseworthy.

Finally, the problem that affected the argument from cowardice may also affect this argument if to say that an act results from patient endurance is to say that it results from a certain motive. To condemn the motive behind an act is to condemn the agent, not the act itself. So, from the fact that a given suicide resulted from a lack of patient endurance, nothing can be determined about the moral permissibility of the act, although our estimation of the agent's moral character may be affected.

However, it is possible that patient endurance is not thought of as a motive behind acts. Perhaps "patient endurance" can be defined without reference to motives. We might try to define it simply as a way of behaving. If some such definition succeeded, which would be surprising, then the objection of the last paragraph would not apply. However, the attempt to condemn suicide on the ground that it manifests a lack of patient endurance would still face the problems mentioned earlier.

(3) The third claim we have to consider asserts that suicide is wrong because to commit suicide is to forgo character development through suffering. It seems clear that the idea that people's characters can develop through suffering is one which frequently finds its way into ordinary life. How many young men have been encouraged to join the armed forces on the ground that "it will make a man of you"?

However, there are limits to this call to suffering. We can admit that certain kinds and degrees of suffering have desirable character-building effects, but this is not true of all suffering. Further, even in cases where suffering does produce some character development, we have to ask whether the cost (suffering) is worth the gain (character development). Let us consider these two issues separately.

Although many people are strengthened by the mental or physical suffering they endure during a war, many return badly in need of psychotherapy. Although many are strengthened by the deaths of their loved ones, many are crushed. Although a psychologically traumatic event (e.g., torture, sexual molestation) may strengthen some, it will drive others into mental institutions or corrupt them morally. How often do the molested become the molesters? These are cases in which suffering, far from having a positive effect on character, actually has a negative effect.

It might be said that although suffering sometimes has a negative effect on character, it presents an *opportunity* for character development; suicide is wrong because the suicide forgoes the *opportunity* for character development through suffering. This assumes that those whose characters have been harmed by intense suffering had the option of developing their characters instead. However, there are numerous instances in which this is not the case; for example, those who become psychotic because of some psychological trauma do not simply choose psychosis over development.

However, let us grant for the moment the obviously false thesis that every instance of suffering has a positive effect on character. Still, we must weigh the positive value of this development against the negative value of the suffering. No one is obliged to achieve some imperceptible improvement in character at the cost of horrendous personal suffering. Not all suffering is worthwhile in terms of character development. The suffering that is worthwhile will have a negative value far outweighed by the positive value of character development. So the greater the quantity of suffering, the greater the character development will have to be if we are obliged to endure that suffering in order to achieve the corresponding character development. The problem that now arises is that in many of the kinds of situations in which one might consider suicide, the apparent quantity of suffering seems to outweigh the benefits in terms of character development. Consider the case of an elderly woman who has just contracted a disease which will cause her to suffer terribly for several years before it kills her. Perhaps there can be some improvement in her character even at this stage in her life, but it seems that this improvement simply would not be valuable enough to require her to endure the suffering.

Conclusion

Having exposed the errors of the major religious and popular arguments against the moral permissibility of suicide, we can go on to consider the more substantial philosophical arguments. As we shall see, they are somewhat more successful. Further, they will pave the way for the position developed in Chapter 3. However, the arguments to be discussed in the next chapter, like the religious and popular arguments of the present chapter, fail to show that all suicide is wrong.

One might object that there are other religious or popular arguments against suicide, or that at least one or more of the arguments discussed in this chapter can be interpreted in yet other ways. However, we have certainly reviewed all the well-known religious arguments and have considered various proposed interpretations of several of them, and we have considered the most well-known popular arguments against suicide. If none of these is successful, then, although it is certainly possible that there is some religious or popular argument against suicide which successfully shows that suicide is always or almost always wrong, it seems extremely unlikely, and no one can justifiably ask that every conceivable argument be taken seriously.

Notes

1. William V. Rauscher, *The Case Against Suicide* (New York: St. Martin's Press, 1981), 60.

2. St. Thomas Aquinas, "The Catholic View," in *Suicide: Right or Wrong?*, ed. John Donnelly (Buffalo: Prometheus Books, 1990), 34.

3. Flavius Josephus, *The Jewish War*, trans. H.St.J. Thackeray (London: William Heinemann Ltd., 1927), vol. 2, 679-81.

4. Aquinas, "The Catholic View," 35; Darrel W. Amundsen, "Suicide and Early Christian Values," in *Suicide and Euthanasia: Historical and Contemporary Themes*, ed. Baruch A. Brody (Dordrecht: Kluwer Academic Publishers, 1989), 142.

5. Glanville Williams, *The Sanctity of Life and the Criminal Law* (New York: Alfred A. Knopf, 1974), 264; Fred Feldman, *Confrontations with the Reaper* (New York: Oxford University Press, 1992), 211-12. In the next section it will be shown that this interpretation of Aquinas is mistaken.

6. Interestingly, Schopenhauer denies (2): "Far from being denial of the will [to live], suicide is a phenomenon of the will's strong affirmation" since the suicide "wills life, and is dissatisfied merely with the conditions on which it has come to him. Therefore he gives up by no means the will-to-live, but merely life." Arthur Schopenhauer, *The World as Will and Representation*, vol. 1, trans. E.F.J. Payne (New York: Dover Publications, Inc., 1969), 398.

7. Margaret P. Battin, *Ethical Issues in Suicide* (Englewood Cliffs: Prentice-Hall, 1982), 54.

8. Williams, *Sanctity of Life*, 250. Also see A. Alvarez, *The Savage God: A Study of Suicide* (New York: Random House, 1970), 72; and Feldman, *Confrontations with the Reaper*, 212.

9. Jerry Jacobs, *The Moral Justification of Suicide* (Springfield: Charles C. Thomas, 1982), 136. This kind of answer would also be given by Schopenhauer; see note 6 above.

10. Feldman, *Confrontations with the Reaper*, 211, interprets Aquinas this way.

11. John Donne, *Biathanatos*, ed. M. Rudick and M.P. Battin (New York: Garland, 1982), lines 1689-97.

12. Tom L. Beauchamp, "Suicide," in *Matters of Life and Death*, 2nd ed., ed. Tom Regan (New York: Random House, 1986), 96.

13. Battin, *Ethical Issues in Suicide*, 56; also Beauchamp, "Suicide," 96.

14. Frederick Copleston, *Aquinas* (Baltimore: Penguin Books, 1955), 221, 223.

15. St. Thomas Aquinas, *Basic Writings of Saint Thomas Aquinas*, vol. 2, ed. Anton C. Pegis (New York: Random House, 1945), 774.

16. Ibid., 775.

17. Beauchamp, "Suicide," 95; also his "An Analysis of Hume's Essay 'On Suicide'," *Review of Metaphysics* 30 (September 1976): 79.

18. Beauchamp, "Suicide," 98.

19. Aquinas, *Basic Writings*, 765-66.

20. Aquinas, "The Catholic View," 34.

21. Ibid.

22. Rauscher, *The Case Against Suicide*, 66.

23. David Lester, *Questions and Answers about Suicide* (Philadelphia: The Charles Press, Publishers, 1989), 2.

24. Maurice Farber, *Theory of Suicide* (New York: Funk & Wagnalls, 1968), 10-11.

25. Battin, *Ethical Issues in Suicide*, 6.

26. Farber, *Theory of Suicide*, 10.

27. Alvarez, *The Savage God*, 51; Amundsen, "Suicide," 77; P.R. Baelz, "Suicide: Some Theological Reflections," in *Suicide: The Philosophical Issues*, ed. M.P. Battin and D.J. Mayo (London: Peter Owen, 1980), 78; Battin, *Ethical Issues in Suicide*, 29; Joseph Fletcher, "Attitudes Toward Suicide," in *Suicide: Right or Wrong?*, ed. John Donnelly, 65; Hume, "Of Suicide," in *Dialogues Concerning Natural Religion and the Posthumous Essays*, ed. Richard Popkin (Indianapolis: Hackett Publishing Co., 1980), 104; Harry Kuitert, "Have Christians the Right to Kill Themselves? From Self-Murder to Self-Killing," in *Suicide and the Right to Die*, ed. J. Pohier and D. Mieth (Edinburgh: T & T Clark, 1985), 104; J. Davis McCaughey, "Suicide: Some Theological Considerations," *Theology* 70 (1967): 63; Terence M. O'Keeffe, "Suicide and Self-Starvation," in *Suicide: Right or Wrong?*, ed. John Donnelly, 120; Arthur Schopenhauer, "On Suicide," in *Parerga and Paralipomena*, vol. 2, trans. E.F.J. Payne

(Oxford: Oxford University Press, 1974), 306; Williams, *The Sanctity of Life*, 249.

28. St. Augustine, *The City of God*, trans. Marcus Dods, in vol. 18 of *Great Books of the Western World*, ed. Robert Maynard Hutchins (Chicago: Encyclopedia Britannica, Inc., 1952), 144.

29. Battin, *Ethical Issues in Suicide*, 33-34; also see Hume, "Of Suicide," 104-5.

30. Amundsen, "Suicide," 95-96.

31. This phrase derives from Battin, *Ethical Issues in Suicide*, 38.

32. Josephus, *The Jewish War*, 681.

33. Aquinas, "The Catholic View," 34.

34. Plato, *Phaedo*, in *The Last Days of Socrates.*, trans. Hugh Tredennick (Middlesex: Penguin, 1954), 62b-c. There is dispute about this passage; see John M. Cooper, "Greek Philosophers on Euthanasia and Suicide," in *Suicide and Euthanasia*, ed. Baruch A. Brody, 15-16; David Novak, *Suicide and Morality* (New York: Scholars Studies Press, Inc., 1975), 8-19.

35. John Locke, *An Essay Concerning the True Original, Extent and End of Civil Government*, in *The English Philosophers from Bacon to Mill*, ed. Edwin A. Burtt (New York: Modern Library, 1939), 405.

36. Ibid.

37. Josephus, *The Jewish War*, 681.

38. Immanuel Kant, "Duties toward the Body in Regard to Life," in *Suicide: Right or Wrong?*, ed. John Donnelly, 52.

39. Ibid., 53.

40. Battin, *Ethical Issues in Suicide*, 43.

41. Rauscher, *The Case Against Suicide*, 37.

42. Hume, "Of Suicide," 101.

43. Ibid.

44. Rauscher, *The Case Against Suicide*, 9.

45. Ibid., 28.

46. Michel Eyquem de Montaigne, *The Essays*, trans. Charles Cotton, in *Great Books of the Western World*, vol. 25, ed. Robert Maynard Hutchins (Chicago: Encyclopedia Britannica, 1952), 167.

47. Hume, "Of Suicide," 102.

48. Aristotle, *Nicomachean Ethics*, trans. W.D. Ross, in *The Basic Works of Aristotle*, ed. Richard McKeon (New York: Random House, 1941), 1116a13-15.

49. Josephus, *The Jewish War*, 679.

50. Amundsen, "Suicide," quotes numerous passages from early Christian writers which express this theme; see 91, 93, 95, 109-12, 114.

51. Augustine, *City of God*, 143.

52. Amundsen, "Suicide," 92.

53. Montaigne, *The Essays*, 167.

54. Immanuel Kant, *Groundwork of the Metaphysic of Morals*, trans. H.J. Paton (New York: Harper Torchbooks, 1964), 66.

CHAPTER 2

PHILOSOPHICAL ARGUMENTS
AGAINST SUICIDE

Unlike the religious arguments considered in the last chapter, the arguments against the moral permissibility of suicide which are considered in the present chapter involve no theological assumptions. They are also of greater philosophical importance. I will consider (a) Kant's arguments based on his ethical theory, (b) various formulations of the argument that suicide is wrong because of the alleged value or sanctity of human life, and (c) other-regarding arguments (i.e., arguments which condemn suicide by appealing to the individual's duties to other persons). I hope to show that none of these arguments establishes the claim that all suicide is morally wrong.

Kant: Universalizability
and Humanity in Oneself

Universalizability and Suicide

In a well-known passage, Kant argued against the moral permissibility of suicide by appealing to one formulation of the "categorical imperative," Kant's principle for determining the permissibility or obligatoriness of actions. The formulation in question commands one to "*Act as if the maxim of your action were to become through your will a universal law of nature.*"[1] Using this principle, Kant considered the case of a man who, sick of life to the point of despair, is pondering suicide:

A man feels sick of life . . . but he [asks] himself
whether taking his own life may not be contrary to
his duty. . . . He now applies the test "Can the
maxim of my action really become a universal law of
nature?" His maxim is "From self-love I make it my
principle to shorten my life if its continuance
threatens more evil than it promises pleasure." The
only further question to ask is whether this principle
of self-love can become a universal law of nature. It
is then seen at once that a system of nature by
whose law the very same feeling whose function
(*Bestimmung*) is to stimulate the furtherance of life
should actually destroy life would contradict itself
and consequently could not subsist as a system of
nature. Hence this maxim cannot possibly hold as a
universal law of nature and is therefore entirely
opposed to the supreme principle of all duty.[2]

Like virtually all of Kant's utterances on substantial
philosophical issues, this passage has aroused numerous scholars
into interpretive action. We will have to examine some of their
claims.

(i) It has been pointed out that Kant's argument here is not
that suicide is wrong because if everyone committed suicide there
would be no one left to do so.[3] As it stands, that argument says
nothing about a *contradiction* in willing the universalization of the
suicide's maxim. Further, it would be very uncharitable to attribute
such an obviously unsound argument to Kant; an analogous
argument would establish the impermissibility of lifelong celibacy.
However, even this interpretation of Kant's argument finds some
support in the *Critique of Practical Reason*, where Kant appears to
argue that suicide is wrong since "such an arrangement [i.e.,
universal law of nature] could not constitute a *permanent* natural
order."[4] Nevertheless, for the reasons just given, we should pursue
other interpretations of Kant.

(ii) Some philosophers have claimed that the contradiction
which Kant finds in the universalization of suicide from self-love is
that the motive of self-love would then sometimes cause one to seek
to preserve one's life, while at other times it would lead one to kill
oneself. It is then correctly pointed out that there is no contradiction

involved; it is not incoherent to suppose that self-love might sometimes cause one to preserve one's life, while at other times (e.g., in conditions of extreme and irremediable pain) it might cause one to kill oneself. The same motive can lead one to perform a certain type of act in a certain type of situation while it might lead one to refrain from that act in another situation.[5]

(iii) A somewhat more plausible reconstruction of Kant's argument can be formulated as follows:[6]

1. If person P acts from self-love and conditions C obtain, then P will commit suicide. (This is the proposed universal law.)

2. If P acts from self-love, then P will not commit suicide; self-love never motivates acts of self-destruction.

3. Supposition: P acts from self-love and conditions C obtain.

4. Therefore, P will commit suicide, and P will not commit suicide.

Here we conclude with a genuine contradiction. However, this argument (in premise 2) interprets Kant as meaning that "it is *factually* true of self-love that it always involves not taking one's life."[7] But surely this interpretation is mistaken since it attributes to Kant the view that no one ever in fact commits suicide from self-love. It seems very unlikely that Kant would deny that people sometimes commit suicide from the motive of self-love; it hardly seems necessary for him to argue repeatedly against an act that no one ever in fact commits.

(iv) What the previous interpretations of Kant's argument ignore is that his reasoning rests on a teleological claim about the "function" or purpose of self-love:[8]

> [Kant] argues that the maxim of arbitrarily destroying one's own life from the motive of self-love, if made a universal law, would generate a teleological contradiction with the already given, natural function or role or purpose . . . of the same self-love "to stimulate the furtherance of life. . . ." Because the maxim under review would then

> generate a world . . . in which the same self-love
> would have two universal but contrary functions--
> both to promote and to destroy one's own life--it
> could not function as a law in a possible moral
> world.[9]

On this view, Kant is not denying that people in fact commit suicide from the motive of self-love. Kant's argument is that the maxim of committing suicide from self-love, when transformed into a universal law, could not form part of a "system of nature." The reason is that the "function" of self-love (i.e., its purpose) always involves the preservation of one's life. A self-love that *always* has self-preservation as its function cannot coherently also have the function of sometimes bringing about self-destruction. If self-preservation is always the function of self-love, then self-love cannot coherently have the additional function of leading to self-destruction. In short, suicide from self-love is wrong because its universalized maxim cannot be part of a coherent system of nature in which the function of self-love always involves self-preservation.

This argument raises many questions. First, the claim that self-love has a "function" or purpose seems quite odd indeed. This view suggests a purposive view of nature, a theme which is repeatedly expressed in the *Groundwork of the Metaphysic of Morals*, where Kant can be found speaking of nature's purposes.[10] Second, even if self-love does have a function of some kind, it is not clear why it can never have self-deliverance from pain through suicide as a function. Just as some authors have asked why self-love could not on some occasions *cause* self-preservation even though on other occasions it might *cause* self-destruction (section (ii) above), one can also ask why self-love cannot have a complex *function*: rather than having self-preservation as its sole function, it might have self-preservation as its function in some contexts and self-destruction as its function in other contexts. The alleged function of self-love might be more complex than Kant supposes. Third, although, as we shall see, Kant opposes all suicide, the present argument, even if sound, would only establish the impermissibility of suicide from self-love. Kant's argument says nothing about other kinds of suicide. Finally, there are also well-known objections to Kant's universalizability criterion: e.g., that Hitler and others seem capable of universalizing the maxim of showing no concern for those who are defeated in battle hardly seems relevant to the issue of whether so acting is permissible. On the other hand, even if one could not universalize the maxim of celibacy, celibacy still seems permissible.

Not only does Kant's argument fail to show the impermissibility of suicides other than those motivated by self-love, it can actually be used to defend the permissibility of certain kinds of suicide. For instance, the terminally ill person who is contemplating suicide as a means of relieving others of the extreme emotional and financial burdens which his illness brings them might act on the following maxim (modelled on Kant's example): "From altruistic motives I make it my principle to shorten my life by means of suicide if its continuance would cause others an enormous amount of suffering." I can see no reason why this maxim cannot be willed as a universal law. Universalized as a law, it would run something like the following: "Whenever anyone is in circumstances in which his continued existence would cause others an enormous amount of suffering (i.e., far more suffering than his death by suicide would cause), he will commit suicide." I cannot find in this any internal contradiction. Nor does it seem impossible for someone to will this (or at least something very much like it) as a universal law of nature.

Consider also the maxim: "Whenever my physical condition is such that I would live for only a brief period, and this period would be marked by unbearable personal suffering, and no one would be seriously affected by my committing suicide, I will commit suicide." I seem to be able to will the universalization of this maxim: "Whenever anyone's physical condition is such that he or she would live for only a brief period, and this period would be marked by unbearable personal suffering, and no one would be seriously affected by the person's suicide, he or she will commit suicide." Others also seem capable of universalizing this maxim.[11] Some have even argued that suicide will soon become the preferred mode of death.[12]

It seems, then, that one of Kant's main arguments against suicide leaves a great deal to be desired. The categorical imperative on which it rests is highly controversial. Further, even if successful, Kant's argument would only show the immorality of one kind of suicide: suicide from self-love; Kant's sweeping condemnation of suicide remains unjustified. Moreover, the present formulation of the categorical imperative seems to show the permissibility of other kinds of suicide. Finally, the teleological character of Kant's argument is problematic; it is unclear why self-love must have a "function," and one cannot plausibly claim that self-love could not have a function more complex than Kant was willing to allow.

Humanity in Oneself and Suicide

Kant bases another anti-suicide argument on an alternative formulation of the categorical imperative. This formulation runs as follows:

> *Act in such a way that you always treat humanity, whether in your own person or in the person of any other, never simply as a means, but always at the same time as an end.*[13]

Using this formulation, Kant argues as follows:

> If . . . [the potential suicide] does away with himself in order to escape from a painful situation, he is making use of a person merely as a *means* to maintain a tolerable state of affairs till the end of his life. But man is not a thing--not something to be used *merely* as a means: he must always in all his actions be regarded as an end in himself. Hence I cannot dispose of man in my person by . . . killing [myself].[14]

Kant's claim is not merely that persons have value; rather, a person is an end "such that in its place we can put no other end to which they should serve *simply* as means."[15] For Kant, a person is a being characterized by the capacity for rationality and autonomy (the capacity to generate and obey moral law). In the case of human beings, this capacity is called "humanity." Humanity is what makes human beings absolutely valuable. The categorical imperative requires that we not treat such beings merely as means; they must always be treated also as ends.

One version of his argument against suicide runs as follows:

A. If one commits suicide in order to avoid painful circumstances, one thereby uses oneself merely as a means.

B. If one uses someone merely as a means, one thereby does something morally wrong.

C. Therefore, if one commits suicide in order to avoid painful circumstances, one thereby does something morally wrong.

I will first state two preliminary objections to this argument. Then an alternative Kantian argument will be considered. First, is it true (as premise A asserts) that committing suicide to avoid painful circumstances involves using oneself merely as a means? It seems not. In committing suicide, one carries out one's own intentions. It is hard to see how carrying out one's own intentions could involve using oneself merely as a means. I cannot be a pawn in my own game. I am not violating my own rights in committing suicide. Second, even if it is possible to use oneself as a mere means, it is not clear that doing so is morally wrong (as premise B entails). Kant's imperative seems plausible (with qualifications) when applied to others--one cannot treat others as mere means. However, it seems at least doubtful that it is wrong to "exploit" oneself independently of the effect which doing so has on others.

However, there is an alternative formulation of the Kantian argument against suicide which may avoid both of these objections:

(a) Every human being is obligated to respect her own humanity (i.e., her capacity for rationality and autonomy).

(b) To commit suicide to avoid pain is to violate this obligation.

(c) Therefore, to commit suicide to avoid pain is morally wrong.

This is how Kant's argument is sometimes understood:

> Suicide (at least suicide for the reasons Kant imagined) is opposed to the principle of humanity as an end in itself . . . because it "throws away" and degrades humanity in oneself. Thus, suicide expresses an attitude that one's nature as a rational,

autonomous person is not of "incomparable worth"
and "above all price." Suicide to end pain, for
example, places cessation of pain, which is a mere
"relative" and "conditioned" value, above rationality
and autonomy, which (Kant says) have worth that
"admits of no equivalent."[16]

Kant's claim is that there is nothing which can have more value for
human beings than the characteristic of humanity (rationality and
autonomy). To place anything else, such as relief from pain, above
humanity in one's own person is to lack respect for humanity. But
humanity in one's own person must be respected. Since committing
suicide involves degrading one's humanity by placing something of
lesser value above humanity, suicide is wrong.

Premise (a) of Kant's argument claims that we are obligated
to respect the humanity we find in ourselves. For Kant, this does not
mean that we should never allow ourselves to be killed:

Humanity in our own person is an object of the
highest esteem and is inviolable in us; rather than
dishonor it, or allow it to be dishonored, man ought
to sacrifice his life. . . . If a man cannot preserve his
life except by dishonoring his humanity, he ought
rather to sacrifice it . . . ; what matters is that, so
long as he lives, man should live honorably and
should not disgrace the dignity of humanity.[17]

One should preserve one's humanity by continuing to live, but not at
the cost of degrading one's humanity. For example, if one had to
choose between being killed and being reduced to a prostitute, one
should, according to Kant, choose death.[18]

The preservation of life is, therefore, not the highest
duty, and men must often give up their lives merely
to secure that they shall have lived honorably.[19]

Kant's position is that "we ought to go on living as long as we can do
so as human beings and honorably."[20] So it seems that premise (a)
of Kant's argument should be clarified by being reformulated as
follows:

(a')   Every human being who can continue living is obligated to do so unless this must involve degrading her own humanity.

Premise (b) of Kant's argument claims that to commit suicide in order to escape from pain violates this duty. The reason runs as follows:

> No matter what torments I have to suffer, I can live morally. I must suffer them all, including the torments of death, rather than commit a disgraceful action.[21]

Since the person committing suicide in order to avoid painful (but not morally degrading) circumstances is in a position to continue living morally, he is obligated to do so. So premise (b) of Kant's argument should read

(b')   To commit suicide to avoid painful (but not morally degrading) circumstances is to violate this obligation (i.e., the obligation mentioned in (a')).

Kant concludes that to commit suicide to avoid painful (but not morally degrading) circumstances is wrong.

This argument and Kant's related claims raise a number of important points:

(1) Far from justifying Kant's sweeping claim that "suicide is in no circumstances permissible"[22] his views actually lead to the conclusion that in certain circumstances suicide is permissible or even obligatory. Some authors have been suspicious of the fact that Kant ignores cases in which the only option to suicide is moral degradation.[23] An example may explain the worry. Suppose, for instance, that I face the following option: I can either commit suicide or I will be brainwashed into becoming a child-molester, where the method of brainwashing is entirely effective. Kant claims that

> If . . . I cannot preserve my life except by disgraceful conduct, virtue relieves me of this duty because a higher duty here comes into play and commands me to sacrifice my life.[24]

In the imagined case, I must either commit suicide or suffer moral
degradation. Since Kant insists that the duty to live honorably
outweighs the duty to preserve one's life, it seems that suicide in the
imagined case is obligatory. The cases Kant has in mind are cases
in which one must either suffer moral degradation or be killed *by
others*.[25] In such cases, he calls for death since the preservation of
life is not the highest duty.[26] In cases in which suicide is the only
alternative to moral degradation, Kant's position seems to require
suicide.

(2) Has Kant even established the impermissibility of suicide
in order to escape from painful (but not morally degrading)
circumstances? The full answer to this question will be implied by
the position taken in the next chapter. However, we can say here
that Kant seems to maintain (e.g., in premise (a')) an implausible
view of the relative values of "humanity" and happiness.[27] According
to Kant, humanity (rationality and autonomy) cannot legitimately be
reduced to achieve any degree of relief from physical or mental
suffering. Kant's view implies that one must never reduce one's
humanity to mitigate any amount of pain in oneself. It seems
implausible to claim that one must endure chronic and profound
suffering even though a reduction in one's humanity might bring
about relief. The claim that, for example, patients suffering the
horrors of certain terminal illnesses should not reduce their agony
by taking a drug that would reduce their capacities for rationality is
implausible at best (wicked at worst). Kant's belief that one is
relieved of the obligation to live *only when* one faces moral
degradation (premise (a')) requires one to prolong one's life, however
meaningless and horrific it might be, if one does not face moral
degradation; no amount of suffering or non-moral degradation has
any bearing whatsoever on whether or not one is permitted to
commit suicide so long as one does not face moral degradation.
Kant's refusal to take seriously anything but moral degradation
seems to be a feature of his theory which can appeal only to the most
fanatical stoic.

(3) Premise (a') of Kant's argument can be criticized on a
second ground. For not only is it doubtful that the prospect of moral
degradation is a necessary condition for being relieved of the duty to
live; it is doubtful that there is a duty to live which is independent
of all one's duties to others. If the duty to live is simply a derived
duty--derived from duties one has towards others (e.g., the duty to

fulfill an important promise)--this opens up the possibility that suicide becomes permissible when those duties to others are absent or insignificant. So, not only does it seem likely that pain and non-moral degradation are relevant to the moral permissibility of suicide (as we saw under (2) above); it is at least unclear that Kant is right in assuming that there is a duty to live which is independent of duties to others.

Kant has failed to justify his sweeping condemnation of suicide. His anti-suicide arguments involve dubious assumptions (e.g., that nature is purposive, that the prospect of moral degradation is required if one is to be relieved of the duty to live) which greatly reduce their plausibility as anti-suicide arguments. Further, far from justifying a universal condemnation of suicide, Kant's remarks entail that suicide is in some circumstances permissible or even obligatory.

However, while the Kantian arguments discussed above fail to show that suicide is always wrong, or even that it is always wrong to commit suicide to avoid painful circumstances, his ideas do suggest a related set of arguments against the moral permissibility of suicide. These arguments proclaim the sanctity or value of life, or at least human life. In the next section these claims will be considered.

The Value of Human Life

It is often said, especially in connection with the problem of abortion, that life, or at least human life, is sacred or that it has absolute value.[28] Proponents of abortion, for example, are accused of failing to recognize the "sanctity of human life" or the supreme value of human beings. The expression "the sanctity of human life" suggests a religious doctrine. It suggests that what makes human lives so precious is the alleged fact that human beings, unlike other animals, have immaterial souls which were created by the deity. However, it is possible to divorce the claim that life has absolute value (in some sense) from any theological assumptions. It can then be considered as a possible principle in a purely secular ethical standpoint.

Suicide, like abortion, is sometimes condemned on the vague ground that to commit suicide is to violate the principle of the sanctity or absolute value of human life. It is claimed with respect to every "rational being" that the "very existence of such a being--its life--will possess a value in itself"; from this it is inferred that "the destruction of even one of these would constitute a moral transgression."[29] The same appeal to the sanctity of human life is made to justify suicide prevention measures; it is claimed that "*every* human life is important, and so *every* human life is to be saved."[30]

It is hard to see how the principle of the sanctity of human life, so construed, can be squared with many practices which we are inclined to regard as permissible or even obligatory. For instance, we are inclined to say that it is permissible to kill in a just war. Likewise, it is permissible to kill in self-defense. With an even greater appearance of paradox, many of those who are most willing to use the rhetoric of the "sanctity of human life" are strongly in favor of capital punishment. So it seems that the claim that human life has "absolute value" is not to be understood as meaning the following:

(1)   It is always wrong to kill a human being.

If the principle did mean this, then it would surely be mistaken.

Perhaps the principle of the sanctity of human life claims only the following:

(2)   It is always wrong to take innocent human life.

But this in itself could not be used to establish the impermissibility of all suicide since it says nothing of suicide among the guilty.

The principle that it is always wrong to take innocent human life also conflicts with other beliefs we are inclined to hold. For instance, the bombing of a certain small town containing innocent people of all ages during a major war might be morally appropriate given the circumstances. Suppose, for instance, that bombing the town in question with conventional weapons is required in order to avoid a nuclear holocaust. (One need not even appeal to such philoso-fiction if it is granted that some bombings of towns during World War II were justified.) It might be claimed that the inhabitants are actually morally guilty since they endorse or at least tolerate the regime which is threatening nuclear devastation. But at least one problem with this claim arises from the fact that young children would be killed in the bombing. Assuming that these children are "innocent" in the appropriate sense (whatever that may be), one cannot claim that it is always wrong to kill innocent human beings and yet claim that the bombing of such a town is justified. In many cases, where the death of one set of innocent human beings is the only means of preventing the killing of a *very much larger* set of innocent human beings, we acknowledge the permissibility of killing innocent human beings. A principle like (2), which at first sight might seem acceptable, does not cohere with many of our moral convictions.[31]

However, in cases like the bombing of a town during a major war, what might incline us to view the action as justified is the fact that more deaths would result if the town is not bombed. So perhaps the principle of the sanctity of human life only commits one to the following principle:

(3)   One should never take innocent human life except when doing so is the only way to avoid the loss of a greater number of innocent human lives; in such cases, one can kill (or let die) the smaller set of innocent human beings.

Aside from the fact that this principle is no longer strong enough to rule out all suicide (since committing suicide may be the act which results in the fewest deaths), it conflicts with some of our most deeply held moral convictions. For example, it would allow a doctor to kill a healthy innocent person in order to use his organs to save several other innocent persons when killing the one person is the only way to save the others. Further, there are cases in which going to war against a certain country is right even though the total amount of death among the innocent is greater than the total that would result from not going to war. Suppose that an evil leader in country X (whose inhabitants are equally vicious) decides that his country will invade country Y, a nation full of innocent and peace-loving people with a just government. X intends to enslave the adult inhabitants of Y, while using the children as means to sexual gratification. If Y surrenders immediately, very few innocent people will die, but the inhabitants of Y will be enslaved and sexually exploited. On the other hand, going to war against X will result in the loss of a large number of innocent human lives. Surely country Y is permitted to defend itself even though many more innocent people would thereby be killed than would be killed by their surrendering or refusing to fight. If so, then (3) proscribes what we are inclined to permit or even prescribe.

Precisely the same objection applies to the following analysis of the sanctity of human life:

(4)   Human life can never be sacrificed in order to bring about or maintain anything other than human life.

In other words, it is always wrong to bring about or allow a human death in order to realize or maintain something other than human lives. One cannot, for instance, kill or allow people to die so that unemployment rates can be reduced. One cannot slaughter the homeless in order to bring about an end of homelessness. Obviously, this principle can be used against many suicides (e.g., suicide to avoid personal pain). However, the example concerning nations X and Y disposes of this principle since it is permissible for Y to defend itself against X in order to spare its inhabitants from slavery and sexual exploitation even though human lives will thereby be sacrificed. Further, if it is admitted that a woman can kill her would-be rapist if doing so is the only way to avoid being raped, then (4) will have to be abandoned. The woman in our imagined case would not be placing an absolute value on the preservation of human life; the rapist's life can be sacrificed even though the rapist had no intention of killing his potential victim and the potential victim realized this.[32] (Restricting (4) to innocent human life would avoid this example, but it would not avoid the earlier example of nations X and Y.)

Perhaps the argument against suicide which appeals to the sanctity of human life is to be understood as ruling out suicide on the basis of the following claim:

(5)   Rational beings are intrinsically valuable.

This is clearly implied by the remark quoted earlier that the "very existence of such a being [i.e., a rational being]--its life--will possess a value in itself."[33]

Proponents of the sanctity of human life usually mean something much stronger than (5) since they frequently appeal to the principle in order to combat the abortion of entities that can hardly be described as rational; the principle would have to be widened to cover potentially rational beings. However, even if (5) is acceptable, it cannot be used as a general argument against suicide unless we assume that it is always wrong to destroy something intrinsically valuable. If it is always wrong to destroy something of intrinsic value, and if committing suicide always involves the destruction of something intrinsically valuable, then suicide is always wrong.

But is it always wrong to destroy something intrinsically valuable? If we assume the truth of (5) we can actually show that this question must be answered negatively. One could argue as follows: rational beings are intrinsically valuable (according to principle (5)); it is sometimes right to destroy rational beings (e.g., in the case of World War II); therefore, it is sometimes right to destroy items of intrinsic value.

After examining various possible ways in which the principle of the sanctity of human life might be formulated, I suspect that under no interpretation will the principle provide a general argument against suicide while also cohering with other strong moral intuitions that we tend to have. Either the principle is too strong by ruling out permissible killings, or it fails to show the wrongness of suicide. In the next chapter, however, more will be said regarding the value of human life and the relevance of this to the moral status of suicide.

Other-Regarding Arguments

In the *Nicomachean Ethics*, Aristotle claimed that the suicide is guilty of "treating the state unjustly."[34] Likewise, Aquinas declared that suicide is morally impermissible since "every part, as such, belongs to the whole." Since "every man is part of the community, and so, as such, he belongs to the community" it follows that "by killing himself he injures the community."[35]

Although I do not endorse the view that people "belong to the community," both Aristotle and Aquinas were groping toward a certain set of important arguments against suicide: other-regarding arguments. In my view, some of these arguments are the best arguments available against suicide in that they point to considerations which show that suicide is not always permissible. Such arguments appeal to the fact that the would-be suicide generally has certain obligations to others. Given these obligations, suicide is impermissible.

In what follows, I will consider two kinds of other-regarding arguments against suicide: those which condemn suicide on the basis of the individual's relations to particular people (family members and friends), and those which condemn suicide on the basis of the individual's relation to society in general.

Individuals: Family Members and Friends

The first step in this argument against suicide is to point out various obvious facts about the effects of suicide on the suicide's family members and friends.[36] There is no denying the fact that these effects can be extremely negative. Family members and friends usually face not only the grief involved in the mere death of the suicide; they also face guilt feelings because the death was a product of suicide. They may, for example, wonder what they did to lead the suicide to embrace death. They may also blame themselves for not taking seriously the suicide's frequent expression of suicidal intentions. In cases where a parent of young children commits suicide, the results can be particularly devastating. Most obviously, the children may have to endure a childhood in poverty and neglect. Further, just as children of divorced parents often blame themselves for the divorce, children of a suicide may blame themselves for the suicide. Further, society is always ready to treat the suicide's relatives and friends as if they really were to blame for the death, whether or not there is any evidence for this. Society may also stigmatize the biological relatives of the suicide on the ground that mental illness must "run in the family." The suicide's biological relatives are then viewed with suspicion.

The suffering that suicide would bring to one's family members and friends is only part of the story. By committing suicide, one may violate certain duties one has on the basis of implicit or explicit past agreements one may have made with one's family members or friends. It has been argued that suicide is wrong when it violates certain *prima facie* duties of "covenant-fidelity"--e.g., duties such as gratitude, promise-keeping, and reparations. For example, in choosing to have children, parents make an implicit promise to provide for them, just as children who are provided for have obligations of gratitude to their parents. Insofar as suicide violates these duties, the right to suicide is overridden.[37] On this view, it would generally be wrong to commit suicide while under the obligations which arise from one's past implicit or explicit promises or any other morally legitimate agreements one has made. If, for example, a healthy single mother commits suicide and thereby abandons a small child, the act would ordinarily be wrong even if it did not bring about significant suffering. Even if the child were adopted by a loving and financially well-off family and never learned that his mother abandoned him by means of suicide, the act would still count as morally wrong because the suicide broke an implicit agreement: the implicit agreement to raise and provide for the child.

In connection with one's family members and friends, then, suicide has been condemned on two grounds: (1) the suffering (e.g., grief, guilt, social rejection and suspicion, etc.) that it causes, and (2) the duties of "covenant-fidelity" one has because of special relationships to one's family members and friends. Of course, one cannot use these considerations against all suicide since some people have no living family members or friends; their suicides, far from causing suffering, may relieve someone of a serious burden or otherwise improve someone's prospects in life: e.g., the suicide of an unliked professor might create an employment opportunity for a deserving young scholar. How much suicide, then, can be ruled out based on considerations pertaining to family members and friends?

(1) It cannot plausibly be claimed that any suicide which would at all increase the suffering of the suicide's family members or friends would be morally wrong. This standard is too strong. It is comparable to the view that it is impermissible to wear a certain shirt if doing so would cause one's spouse a slight degree of embarrassment. Such a standard is overly narrow since it totally ignores the agent's self-interest. Likewise, one is not morally

forbidden to pursue a career in philosophy simply because one's family members or friends find this somewhat distressing.

(2) It might be suggested that if the suffering one would cause one's family members or friends outweighs whatever suffering one would avoid by suicide, committing suicide would be wrong. But this also seems too strong. Consider a case in which Jones is suffering from intense and irremediable pain which adds up to 100 units on some hypothetical suffering scale. Jones has, say, 1,000 family members and friends. If he commits suicide, the total amount of suffering they will endure as a result will add up to 110 units. However, no one relative or friend suffers very much. On the contrary, each suffers hardly at all. Given such conditions, it seems that Jones is not prohibited from committing suicide because of the suffering that the act would bring his family members and friends. The reason is that in other contexts people are morally permitted to act in ways that bring their family members and friends a greater amount of suffering than the agent avoids by so acting. Suppose that by pursuing a career in philosophy I am avoiding 10 units of suffering (e.g., the suffering that comes with having to earn a living in a way I find less rewarding). However, my family members and friends are somewhat distressed by my career choice. It strikes them as economically irrational, and the subject seems to them to be nothing more than so much sophistry and illusion. Suppose that collectively my career choice brings my numerous relatives and friends 11 units of suffering and that my decision does not cause any one relative or friend any significant distress. Surely my choice is not immoral simply because it brings my relatives and friends more suffering than I avoid by pursuing a career in philosophy.

(3) It might be suggested that if committing suicide would bring any *one* relative or friend more suffering than the would-be suicide would avoid by means of self-destruction, then suicide would be morally wrong. If, for example, Smith's suicide would cause one of his relatives or friends 10 units of suffering, while Smith avoids only 9.9 units of suffering by killing himself, then the present principle would say that Smith is not morally permitted to commit suicide.

However, I think even this standard is too strong. The reason again is that we are not willing to accept an analogous standard in other cases. For example, imagine that two close friends, Smith and Jones, are philosophy professors. Smith decides to read the works of a third philosopher who is considered by Jones to be a despicable charlatan. Jones is so annoyed that he cannot help but suffer 2 units on our hypothetical suffering scale. However, refraining from reading the works would have cost Smith only 1.5 units. Surely in the case thus described, Smith does not act wrongly in reading the works simply because the suffering (in the form of annoyance) that this causes Jones outweighs the suffering that Smith avoids by reading the works.

Or suppose that Smith decides to part his hair a certain way even though the annoyance he would have had to endure by refraining from parting it in that way is outweighed by a friend's distaste for the new style. Nevertheless, Smith is not doing anything wrong simply by parting his hair in this way.

What these examples show is that we do not find it morally objectionable for someone to act in a certain way simply because he thereby causes a relative or friend a degree of suffering that outweighs the degree which the agent would have suffered by not acting as he did. Therefore, the principle concerning suicide under consideration is mistaken.

Problems also face the attempt to rule out suicide by appealing to the would-be suicide's obligations of "covenant-fidelity" toward his relatives and friends. Clearly, there are limits to our obligations to thank our relatives and friends. There are also limits to our obligations to keep our promises to them.

Despite these problems, the appeal to one's relatives and friends obviously counts against the permissibility of certain suicides; it is at least sometimes wrong to commit suicide because of considerations pertaining to the suicide's family and friends. But when?

It would, I think, be folly to attempt to give a *precise* answer to this question. First, our moral intuitions concerning how much suffering we can legitimately impose on our family and friends are not precise. We know that it is wrong to inflict deep suffering upon them without strong reasons. On the other hand, we know that we have certain rights which we are entitled to exercise even if this will cause our family members or friends some suffering. But our moral intuitions are not sufficiently sharp to allow us to specify the exact limits of our obligation to refrain from causing suffering to our family members and friends. Second, the limits of our obligations of covenant-fidelity are equally unclear. Even if one could, somehow, measure something like inconvenience, it is still unclear just how inconvenient keeping a promise would have to be before one is no longer obliged to keep it.

Before saying anything more about this problem, I want to turn to the other class of other-regarding considerations against suicide. As we shall see, the same problem arises with respect to these.

Society in General

Suicide might be condemned on the basis of the potential suicide's alleged duties to society in general. It might be claimed that even when the potential suicide has no obligations to particular persons, such as relatives and friends, he might still have obligations to society in general. Perhaps one's obligations to the state are sufficient to rule out suicide. Given that one can have obligations to society in general, these obligations may be thought to show that suicide is wrong.

For instance, it might be said that suicide is wrong because each person plays a certain role in society; each person functions as a cog in the wheels of society. To commit suicide is to abandon one's role, thereby hurting society.[38]

Naturally, this has no force in a society marked by growing unemployment and by employment positions that can be filled by virtually any adult or at least by numerous available adults. The unemployed do not hurt society by abandoning their posts, for they have no posts. Nor do the millions who are easily replaceable damage society by abandoning their posts; thousands more are eager to fill the void. Indeed, very few of us (if any) could claim to be irreplaceable. At best, this argument would establish the impermissibility of committing suicide when one's suicide would bring about serious harm to one's society. If, for instance, one were the only military officer capable of saving one's community from occupation and extermination by the Nazis, it would be wrong to commit suicide prior to doing so.

However, as Hume pointed out in a well-known pro-suicide argument, one's continued existence may constitute a significant burden to society. If the burden to society is extreme enough, "my resignation of life must not only be innocent but laudable."[39]

An alternative argument (a variant of which might be used with respect to individuals) might claim that it is virtually always wrong to commit suicide because it is virtually always possible to do something good for society instead. One ought to refrain from suicide if one can otherwise do good for society; suicide is wrong since it deprives society of whatever good the suicide might otherwise have done. "Doing good" here means not only sparing society of suffering (as in the Nazi occupation example); it means increasing the happiness in society.

Battin objects to this "deprivation-of-good" argument on the ground that the principle that individuals have an obligation to do good (as against simply preventing evil), even if true, is "not one of utter self-sacrifice":

> Someone whose life has already reached such excesses of misery that he is considering ending it would hardly be obligated to continue that misery-filled life in order to do good for others.[40]

However, she does not consider cases in which an individual is in a position to do good for society, is not suffering from some painful physical or mental condition, and will not in the foreseeable future be suffering from such a condition. Admittedly, this kind of suicide is atypical, but one can think of cases in which people commit suicide in order to make political statements. Does the deprivation-of-good argument establish the impermissibility of suicide in such cases?

The negative answer to this question is, I think, the correct answer. Even if we admit the claim that there are duties to do good (as against duties to refrain from doing or allowing evil) to others, we attach very little weight to these duties; we allow an individual's rights to do certain things to override alleged duties to benefit others. For instance, it seems permissible in ordinary circumstances to devote one's life to the pursuit of highly abstract mathematical knowledge even though this knowledge will not benefit others. The mathematician could benefit others by using her abilities in other ways; she could, for instance, spend more time teaching children basic mathematics, an activity she does not despise. Nevertheless, it seems permissible for her to devote her time to increasing her own mathematical knowledge. Likewise, an individual is permitted to spend an afternoon in a museum even though he could have worked in a homeless shelter instead. It is morally permissible for one to engage in a certain activity even though an alternative activity would have benefitted society to a higher degree and would not have involved much sacrifice on one's part.

Clearly, it would almost certainly be wrong to commit suicide if by committing suicide one deeply hurt one's society. On the other hand, as Hume pointed out, our obligations to do good "have certainly some bounds; I am not obliged to do a small good to society at the expence of a great harm to myself."[41]

Here we reach the very same problem that we faced in connection with relatives and friends: What are the limits of an individual's obligations to others? It seems to me impossible to give a precise, plausible, and non-arbitrary answer to this question. Any very precise answer, such as one that appeals to precise quantitative relations between happiness and suffering (whether these are actually measurable or not), can be shown to be arbitrary; it will give the impression of being a mere stipulation. Analogously, there is a bald/not-bald distinction, but any attempt to say that some precise number of hairs marks the distinction will be arbitrary. The distinction between cases in which one's rights outweigh one's duties to others and cases in which this does not occur is of the same sort; although there is a distinction, it has no precise boundaries. What this means for our inquiry is that we shall have to be satisfied with saying that (a) a suicide may be wrong because of the agent's obligations to others, (b) there are some clear instances in which this is the case, but (c), unfortunately, no precise and plausible criterion is available which sets the limits of the agent's obligations to others.

Even though no precise criterion determining the limits of our obligations to others has been established, in considering whether or not to commit suicide one must consider the likely consequences for other individuals and for society in general. Further, one must keep in mind one's obligations based on implicit or explicit past agreements, even though the limits of such obligations are equally unclear. Of course, much more thought will usually be required with respect to one's family members and friends since it is only in rare cases that one's suicide has significant implications that extend to society as a whole. In the next chapter, we will have to ask whether anything other than our duties to others is relevant to the moral status of suicide.

Conclusion

The Kantian arguments fail to establish the moral impermissibility of all suicide. They involve controversial assumptions which greatly reduce their plausibility as anti-suicide arguments, and Kant's remarks can even be used to vindicate suicide in some cases. Kant failed to justify his sweeping condemnation of suicide.

Likewise, the argument against suicide which appeals to the sanctity of human life seems very dubious. We found that the principle of the sanctity of human life is either highly questionable (if not obviously false) or insufficient to support a general condemnation of suicide, or both.

Finally, we considered other-regarding arguments against suicide. While none of these establishes the wrongness of all suicide, we admitted that much suicide is morally wrong given the suicide's duties to others. However, there are limits to our duties to others, and, in certain situations, it is arguable that duties to others render suicide obligatory. These claims pave the way for the discussions in the next chapter.

Notes

1. Immanuel Kant, *Groundwork of the Metaphysic of Morals*, trans. H.J. Paton (New York: Harper Torchbooks, 1964), 89, [421]. In referring to the *Groundwork*, numbers in brackets refer to Royal Prussian Academy page numbers, which can be found in the margins of several translations of Kant's ethical works.
2. Ibid., [422].
3. Ibid., 137.

4. Immanuel Kant, *Critique of Practical Reason and Other Writings in Moral Philosophy*, trans. Lewis White Beck (Chicago: University of Chicago Press, 1949), 154, emphasis added.

5. Richard Brandt, "The Morality and Rationality of Suicide," in *Suicide: Right or Wrong?*, ed. John Donnelly (Buffalo: Prometheus Books, 1990), 191; David Ross, *Kant's Ethical Theory* (Oxford: Oxford University Press, 1969), 46.

6. See Ronald Glass, "The Contradictions in Kant's Examples," *Philosophical Studies* 22 (1971): 67.

7. Ibid., 67, emphasis added.

8. J. Kemp, "Kant's Examples of the Categorical Imperative," in *Foundations of the Metaphysics of Morals with Critical Essays*, ed. R.P. Wolff (New York: Bobbs-Merrill, 1969), 234; David Novak, *Suicide and Morality* (New York: Scholars Studies Press, 1975), 86; Roger Sullivan, *Immanuel Kant's Moral Theory* (Cambridge: Cambridge University Press, 1989), 186-87.

9. Sullivan, *Immanuel Kant's Moral Theory*, 186-87.

10. Kant, *Groundwork*, 64, [396]; 97, [430]; 100, [432].

11. Mary Rose Barrington, "Apologia for Suicide," in *Suicide: The Philosophical Issues*, ed. M.P. Battin and D.J. Mayo (London: Peter Owen, 1980), 90-103.

12. Robert Kastenbaum, "Suicide as the Preferred Way of Death," in *Suicidology: Contemporary Developments*, ed. Edwin S. Shneidman (New York: Grune and Stratton, 1976), 425.

13. Kant, *Groundwork*, 96, [429].

14. Ibid., 97, [429].

15. Ibid., 96, [428].

16. Thomas Hill, "Self-Regarding Suicide: A Modified Kantian View," *Suicide and Life-Threatening Behavior* 13 (Winter 1983): 263. While Hill rejects Kant's view, he claims that "*A morally ideal person will value life as a rational, autonomous agent for its own sake, at least provided that the life does not fall below a certain threshold of gross, irremediable, and uncompensated pain and suffering.*" However, as Hill explicitly and repeatedly notes, this principle says nothing about the *permissibility* of suicide, which is my concern here. Further, Hill, unlike Kant, does not oppose all suicide; in fact, he points out that various kinds of suicide are consistent even with being a morally ideal person.

17. Immanuel Kant, "Duties towards the Body in Regard to Life," in *Suicide: Right or Wrong?*, ed. John Donnelly (Buffalo: Prometheus Books, 1990), 54.

18. Ibid., 55.

19. Ibid., 55.

20. Ibid., 52.

21. Ibid., 54.

22. Ibid., 50; see also 51.

23. Tom Beauchamp, "Suicide in the Age of Reason," in *Suicide and Euthanasia: Historical and Contemporary Themes*, ed. Baruch Brody (Dordrecht: Kluwer Academic Publishers, 1989), 211.

24. Kant, "Duties towards the Body," 55.

25. Ibid., 53, 55.

26. Ibid., 55.

27. Hill, "Self-Regarding Suicide," 264.

28. The principle of the sanctity of human life may commit one to "speciesism." See Peter Singer, "Unsanctifying Human Life," in *Ethical Issues Relating to Life and Death*, ed. John Ladd (New York: Oxford University Press, 1979); Jonathan Glover, *Causing Death and Saving Lives* (London: Penguin Books: 1977), 50.

29. Eike-Henner Kluge, *The Practice of Death* (New Haven: Yale University Press, 1975), 130.

30. Erwin Ringel, "Suicide Prevention and the Value of Human Life," in *Suicide: The Philosophical Issues*, ed. M.P. Battin and D.J. Mayo (London: Peter Owen, 1980), 208.

31. For other objections to (2), see Margaret P. Battin, *Ethical Issues in Suicide* (Englewood Cliffs: Prentice Hall, 1982), 116-17.

32. Some have denied that such killing is justifiable: Robert Young, "What Is So Wrong with Killing People?," *Philosophy* 54 (1979): 520.

33. Kluge, *The Practice of Death*, 130.

34. Aristotle, *Nicomachean Ethics*, trans. W.D. Ross, in *The Basic Works of Aristotle*, ed. Richard McKeon (New York: Random House, 1941), 1138a10-13.

35. St. Thomas Aquinas, "The Catholic View," in *Suicide: Right or Wrong?*, ed. John Donnelly (Buffalo: Prometheus Books, 1990), 34.

36. David Lester, *Questions and Answers about Suicide* (Philadelphia: The Charles Press, 1989), 160.

37. Karen Lebacqz and H. Tristram Engelhardt, "Suicide," in *Death, Dying, and Euthanasia*, ed. Dennis Horan and David Mall (Frederick: Aletheia Books, 1980), 690. Lebacqz and Engelhardt allow an exception: the "symbolic protest" suicide.

38. Battin claims that this is one of Plato's implicit arguments against suicide. Battin, *Ethical Issues in Suicide*, 83, note 21.

39. David Hume, "Of Suicide," in *Dialogues Concerning Natural Religion and the Posthumous Essays*, ed. Richard Popkin (Indianapolis: Hackett Publishing Co., 1980), 103-4.

40. Battin, *Ethical Issues in Suicide*, 87.

41. Hume, "Of Suicide," 103.

CHAPTER 3

FROM PERMISSIBLE TO OBLIGATORY SUICIDE

The most fundamental ethical question concerning suicide is: when, if ever, is it morally permissible to commit suicide? Is suicide always wrong? If not, under what kinds of conditions is it permissible? For it is certainly not permissible in all circumstances to commit suicide.

Although the question concerning the moral permissibility of suicide is the most fundamental question we face, we will also have to address a more disturbing question which is less frequently asked but which is equally important: when, if ever, is suicide morally obligatory? Can morality ever require one to commit suicide? If so, under what kinds of circumstances?

We will first consider the conditions under which suicide becomes morally permissible. What obligations limit the permissibility of suicide? What rights tend to make the action permissible? The possibility that suicide may in some circumstances become morally required will then be considered.

Permissible Suicide

I propose to defend the view that duties to others which would be violated by suicide constitute the only consideration that limits the permissibility of suicide. When no such duties are present, suicide is permissible. The permissibility of suicide in the face of duties to others derives from certain individual rights which may override the agent's duties to others. A particular suicide, then, is morally permissible if and only if *it does not involve violating a duty or set of duties to others which overrides the rights which would otherwise permit suicide*. Suicide, then, can be called a "derived

57

right," a right which is derived from other, more general, rights (e.g., the right to free oneself from suffering, the right to act as one sees fit, etc.). Although one might assume the existence of a basic or fundamental (i.e., non-derived) right to suicide, doing so would simply beg the question against the anti-suicide camp. Further, there is no need to assume the existence of a fundamental right to suicide if it can be shown that certain already recognized rights can sometimes justify suicide. In what follows, I will frequently speak of an overrideable "right to suicide." This is to be understood as a convenient way of referring to the overrideable derived right to commit suicide, an overrideable right which exists as a function of other, more general, rights.

Two views which deliver universal judgments on the moral status of suicide will have to be rejected: the view that all suicide is morally permissible, and the view that suicide is always wrong. Contrary to the ultra-permissive view that all suicide is morally permissible, duties to others can override the rights which might otherwise justify suicide. Thus, I do not provide a blanket defense of suicide. On the other hand, certain rights which would justify suicide can override one's duties to others, and in such cases suicide is permissible. Thus, ultra-conservatism with respect to suicide is also mistaken; suicide is not always morally wrong. On the contrary, as we shall see, suicide even seems morally obligatory in certain cases.

According to our criterion, the permissibility of a particular suicide is a function of the answer to the following question: does the individual's duty or set of duties to others override the rights that would otherwise justify suicide? A particular suicide will be permissible when and only when this question receives a negative answer. This must be distinguished from two alternative views.

First, the claim here is not to be confused with the assertion that all suicides which do not *harm* others are morally permissible. That principle mistakenly ignores any duty one may have toward others besides the duty not to harm them. Since we have duties to others which are distinct from the duty to refrain from harming them (e.g., the duty not to break one's promises), a suicide may not harm others while violating some duty other than that of non-maleficence. In those cases where the violated duty overrides the rights that would otherwise permit suicide, that act is morally impermissible.

Second, our claim is not to be confused with the converse thesis that no morally permissible suicides harm others. That thesis is also mistaken; sometimes a right which justifies suicide, like one's right to perform other acts, overrides one's duty not to harm others. I am morally allowed to make certain decisions with respect to my life even though they may involve some harm to others. For example, I may be morally permitted to take a job in another state even though this would bring some emotional harm to my family members and friends. Ordinarily, I am morally permitted to accept a promotion, even though my doing so will cause someone else to be deprived of a promotion.

The idea that self-destructive behavior could be morally permissible on the basis of rights (even though overrideable ones) should come as no surprise. Consider other acts which are known to reduce one's lifespan. Suppose that I am considering taking a job which I know will reduce my lifespan by several years. For instance, I may be considering a position in a country whose inhabitants inevitably have shorter lifespans because of various environmental factors. Although I could take a position in a healthier environment, I have the right to take the position in the less healthy environment, even though I know this will cost me a few years, so long as I do not thereby violate overriding duties to others. Even if there is no doubt whatsoever that by taking a position in such an environment I will shorten my life, I have a right to do so, assuming I do not thereby violate overriding duties to others.

Likewise, suppose it is discovered that smoking a certain brand of cigarettes will necessarily cause a reduction in one's lifespan, assuming one would otherwise die a "natural death." Smoking this brand would still be within one's rights, so long as one does not thereby violate overriding duties to others. One's action might be grossly irrational from the standpoint of self-interest, but it would not count as morally wrong.

What these and other examples show is that we do not claim that an action is not within one's rights simply because of its self-destructive or self-harming aspects. Such factors may lead us to consider the act irrational from the standpoint of the individual's self-interest, but whether it is permissible or not is unaffected. Instead, the actions are considered morally wrong in so far as they violate overriding duties to others. I may smoke the brand of cigarettes in question as I see fit, but only if I do not thereby violate overriding duties to others; I am not, for example, justified in smoking in an atmosphere in which others would be seriously negatively affected by my doing so.

Naturally, there are objections to treating suicide in the way described above. Before considering the specific rights that permit suicide, these objections should be considered, since they will allow us to throw further light on our principle, thus paving the way for the more detailed considerations raised later.

Margaret Battin, who is easily the most prolific contemporary philosopher concerned with the ethical issues raised by suicide, has rejected views like the one I have endorsed. I will consider her objections first and later concentrate on others.

(i) Battin objects that

> to treat suicide as a right which can be overridden
> by other duties and obligations to other persons may
> provide unequal treatment for individuals whose
> grounds for suicide are the same, but who differ in
> their surrounding circumstances. Of two persons
> afflicted with the same terminal illness, for instance,
> one might have a right to suicide while the other's
> right is overridden, if one is free from family
> relationships and the other is not, even though the
> reasons for the suicide might be the same.[1]

We shall have to agree that our account does lead to the unequal treatment that Battin fears; where person A's duties to others override his right to suicide, his suicide is wrong on our account, even though his grounds for suicide may be identical to person B's, whose suicide is not wrong since he does not have overriding duties to others.

However, this consequence is not in the least surprising. Clearly, we are quite willing to judge the actions of two persons differently depending on their relations to others, even though their reasons for acting are identical. Two people might take separate day-long drives in the woods simply in order to enjoy the lovely scenery. One might be judged to have done nothing wrong while the other is condemned; we might, for example, discover that while the first person has no children and is not relied on by others, the second left a seriously ill infant alone for the entire day. Likewise, one person may be morally permitted to emigrate while another is not, simply because the latter, unlike the former, has overriding duties to others. There is nothing at all unusual about the idea that two instances of the same type of act done for the same reason may be judged differently based on the agents' duties to others.

(ii) Battin adds a further point:

> If suicide is a right overrideable . . . on the basis of duties and obligations to others, two potential suicides whose interpersonal relationships and commitments to others are similar may have the same right, or lack thereof, to kill themselves, even though they have vastly different reasons for doing so.[2]

We can refer to examples which Battin employs elsewhere to clarify the issue. Imagine two people, an old woman considering suicide to avoid the agony involved in her terminal illness, and a teenager considering suicide because his favorite television show was cancelled.[3]

On our account, different suicides based on reasons which differ in quality *may* have the same moral status, depending on whether or not the suicides violate overriding duties the agent had toward others. However, Battin has ignored the factors that allow one's right to commit suicide to override one's duties to others. As we shall discuss below, the fact that one is in deep and unremediable pain is a prominent consideration in determining whether one's right to commit suicide outweighs one's duties to others. Our account does not have the absurd consequence that Battin imagines: namely, that all suicides of persons with identical relations to others (i.e., identical duties to others) have the same moral status. The reason is that whether duties to others override one's right to suicide is a function not only of one's relations to others, but also of intrinsic features of one's life (e.g., whether or not one is in unremediable agony). Assuming that the old woman and the teenager in Battin's examples have similar relations to others, there can still be a difference in the moral status of their suicides based on the fact that one was suffering from unremediable pain while, presumably, the other was not; the strength of one's right to commit suicide depends in part on such factors as intense suffering.

The following example illustrates the point that two people with identical relations to others can commit the same type of act for different reasons while the moral evaluations of their acts differ. Jones and Smith want to take two-week trips to Russia. Jones's reason is that he wants to see how long the lines are at the grocery stores. Smith's reason is that he is suffering from a painful illness that can be cured only in a Moscow hospital. To simplify matters, we can stipulate that the only relevant fact pertaining to others is that each man has a small daughter who would be significantly negatively affected by the two-week absence of her father. In such a case, it makes perfect sense to say that Jones is not permitted to go to Russia because of his obligations to his daughter, while Smith may be permitted to do so, depending on the seriousness of the harm his daughter would have to endure because of his two-week absence. Even though both men are considering taking two-week trips to Russia, and even though they have identical relations to others, the moral status of their potential actions may differ. Likewise, our account does not involve the formula that Battin imagines: namely, the formula "Same relations to others; so same moral status." As we shall discuss more fully below, whether one's duties to others override one's right to commit suicide depends in part on characteristics of one's own life.

(iii) Battin claims that the "real deficiency" of a view like that defended here is that on such a view

> it will be very difficult to show why, in any case in which others are at all adversely affected, the right to suicide is not always almost immediately overridden. . . . Suicide may be a right, but only a right as substantial as the right to pick one's nose: something you may do just if nobody minds.[4]

Battin holds that a view which restricts permissible suicides in terms of duties to others cannot explain why the suicidal option is not overridden whenever others are "*at all* adversely affected" (emphasis added). However, our freedom to commit suicide in order to avoid extreme, enduring, and unremediable pain is not overridden the instant others would be *at all* negatively affected, just as one's freedom to accept a position in another state is not overridden simply because others would be negatively affected to some degree.

As we shall see below, the rights that justify suicide in certain circumstances are quite general and clearly more weighty than the alleged right to pick one's nose; suicide is not something one may do "just if nobody minds," just as emigrating is not something one may do just if nobody minds.[5]

(iv) Elsewhere Battin very briefly adds that an account like ours "provides no settled account of what particular circumstances might override the right to suicide."[6] Presumably, the reason is that an abstract formula cannot provide an easy answer to the question facing the potential suicide in a real life situation: "May I commit suicide in these particular circumstances?"

Obviously, Battin is correct. The principle that suicide is a derived right limited by overriding duties to others does not remove the difficulty of knowing whether or not one's suicide would be morally acceptable. However, this does not show the falsity of the principle under consideration, just as utilitarianism is not refuted by the mere fact that it is extremely difficult to determine the consequences in terms of general utility of all the actions which one might perform. Unless one assumes that a moral principle, to be true, must be easy to apply, the fact that our principle is not easily applied does not show it to be false.

Nevertheless, Battin is correct in demanding that our account be brought down from the dizzying heights of philosophical abstraction to the concrete level of real-life concerns. This task will occupy us below, where we will consider the rights and circumstances which justify suicide in the face of duties to others that would be violated by suicide. As we shall see, however, our principle does not yield a mechanical solution to the ethical dilemmas involved in suicide.

(v) Battin is also uncomfortable with the alleged fact that

an account which restricts one's right to end one's life in cases in which doing so will have bad consequences for others [i.e., consequences bad enough to override the suicidal option] may seem to oblige us to hold, in consistency, that one is obliged to end one's life in cases where the consequences would be good.[7]

The idea that suicide could be obligatory is clearly a disturbing one. Some have even claimed that "any view which makes a suicide obligatory is wrong."[8] Later in this chapter I will defend the view that suicide may be obligatory in certain kinds of cases. Admittedly, some may be as disturbed as Battin is by this claim, but I hope to show that there is nothing implausible in this idea. For the present, however, we can make the following observations.

First, the view defended here is that duties to others may render an act of suicide impermissible. This does not entail that potential benefits to others may make an act of suicide obligatory. Analogously, duties to others may render smoking in certain situations (e.g., in crowded elevators) impermissible, but it does not follow that benefits which others would derive from one's smoking (e.g., financial gain) may make smoking obligatory. Even assuming that there is a duty to benefit others beyond what is involved in the mere elimination of suffering, it is highly implausible to suggest that such a duty could require self-destructive behavior. This claim is consistent with the thesis that duties to others (e.g., the duty to refrain from causing suffering) may render a case of suicide impermissible.

Second, although a more complete discussion of obligatory suicide will have to wait, I can say that it seems to me that any plausible moral theory must allow for obligatory suicide. The reason is that it is easy to construct examples in which it seems clear that a person is morally required to commit suicide. For instance, if Smith knows how to manufacture nuclear missiles, and he is captured by the forces of an evil dictator who is committed to inaugurating a nuclear holocaust, and Smith will otherwise be given a drug which will guarantee that he tells all, it seems to me that he is obliged to commit suicide. If other varieties of self-sacrifice may be morally required, why not self-sacrificial suicide?

In short, my response to the present objection is twofold. (a) The view that duties to others sometimes make suicide impermissible does not by itself entail that benefits that others might receive from one's suicide may make suicide obligatory. (b) The idea that suicide can be obligatory is not as implausible as it may seem at first sight. In fact, any correct moral principle should allow for the possibility of obligatory suicide.

(vi) Paul-Louis Landsberg, who once considered suicide until having a religious experience while in the hands of the Nazis, also suggests an objection to any view which would limit the permissibility of suicide by reference to others:

> It is purely and simply antipersonalist to try to decide such an intimately personal question as to whether or not I have the right to kill myself by reference to society. Suppose I die a little sooner or a little later, what has that to do with society, to which, in any case, I belong for so short a space?[9]

The Stoic philosopher Seneca also expressed the view that suicide is a purely personal decision which cannot be condemned on the basis of the suicide's relations to others. This claim is meant to support a very permissive thesis with respect to suicide:

> Every man ought to make his life acceptable to others besides himself, but his death to himself alone. The best form of death is the one we like. . . .[10]

We shall have to admit that the decision as to whether or not to commit suicide is "personal" in the sense that it is a decision about oneself. However, suicide is rarely "personal" in the sense that it has no significant consequences for others, either in the form of having to endure suffering or in the form of having their rights violated. For example, suicide may in some instances involve the abandonment of small children for no good reason. In such a case, it would be absurd to defend the act on the ground that suicide is a purely personal decision.

Consider the analogous claim that the decision to have a sex-change operation is "purely personal." Admittedly, it may sometimes happen that such a decision is purely personal, but if the would-be transsexual is married, it may not be a purely personal decision at all. Even though the operation would be performed only on the body of the would-be transsexual, the decision will ordinarily not be a purely personal affair. Likewise, even if the would-be suicide is killing only himself (some suicides might kill themselves in ways that kill others), it does not follow that his decision to do so is a purely personal matter.

(vii) Another pro-suicide argument which is similar to the claim that the decision to commit suicide is a purely personal matter asserts that since one's life is one's own, one may do with it as one pleases, even if that involves suicide. My life, it is said, is my property. Consequently, I may do with it as I please, even if I should decide to destroy it, just as I may destroy my violin if I desire to do so. One might claim that the right to die transcends the claims of one's family or society since one's life is one's property.[11] An ultra-liberal version of this view would deny our claim that other-regarding considerations limit the permissibility of suicide.

Some philosophers have questioned the coherence of the idea that a person's life is her property on the following ground:

> What we own--in any full-blooded sense of that term-
> -we can disown, give away, sell, or otherwise dispose
> of so that it becomes the property of someone else.
> We cannot do this with our lives. Therefore whatever
> the unique relationship this bears to us, it cannot be
> one of ownership.[12]

But what about common expressions like "It's my life," "Jones gave his life for the cause," and "You're throwing your life away"? Such expressions, and numerous others, seem to suggest that the notion that one's life is one's property is not absurd after all. Battin, who also rejects the view that one's life is one's property, claims that such expressions are mere metaphors.[13] In support of this view, she cites the fact that in ordinary property-destruction, the owner of the property continues to exist, while, by definition, in suicide one does not survive the alleged property-destruction.

An even more basic complaint one might raise about the thesis that one's life is one's property is simply that "life" is not an entity of any kind, unlike our other possessions. Even the slave-owner does not own his slave's life or his existence; what he owns is simply the slave. So the concealed meaning behind the claim that one's life is one's property must be that one's person is one's property; I own, not my life, but my person. Of course, destroying a life and destroying a person may be identical, but the distinction between a person and his life may make the thesis under consideration more intelligible since, presumably, a person, like ordinary possessions, is an entity of some sort, while life is not.

To avoid unnecessary digressions, let us assume, despite Battin and others, that it makes sense to say that people own themselves; I, for example, am my own property. Does it follow that suicide is always permissible? That others are irrelevant to the moral status of the act?

I think these questions must be answered negatively. The reason is that it is sometimes morally wrong to destroy one's property given one's duties to others. Suppose I have promised to give my violin to Jones. Although I still own the violin, I am not permitted to destroy it without good reasons (i.e., reasons strong enough to override my obligation to Jones) since I have promised to give him the instrument. Likewise, if I have promised to "give my person" to someone else (e.g., as in marriage), I am not morally permitted to commit suicide prior to this alleged transference of property without good reasons (i.e., reasons strong enough to override my commitment). Finally, suppose that I own your pacemaker, and although you could replace it, doing so would involve deep and enduring physical and mental suffering for you and mental anguish of various sorts for your family and friends. Surely I am not morally permitted to deprive you of the pacemaker for no good reason, even though I own it. The reason is that doing so would violate an overriding duty to others: namely, the duty not to cause deep pain and suffering without good reason. So, even though I own an object, I am not always morally permitted to do what I please with it; other-regarding factors limit even my rights with respect to my property. Thus, even if it makes sense to say that people own themselves, this does not give rise to an ultra-permissive position on the moral status of suicide. Morally speaking, I cannot do whatever I like with my property.

(viii) As noted in the last chapter, suicide is often condemned by appealing to the value of human life. We found that the obscure principle of the "absolute value" or "sanctity" of human life cannot plausibly provide a general objection to suicide. But one may still wonder whether the view presented here simply denies value to life. Do I mean to say that life is worthless?

Presumably, the question as to whether "life" is worthless concerns whether conscious awareness of some sort is worthless. Apparently, we are not to equate "life" in the above question with "being alive." So we can restate the question in this way: is conscious awareness worthless?

I think not. However, that does not show that all suicide is morally wrong. Pleasure may have intrinsic value, but that does not imply that I am obliged to continue experiencing a certain pleasure; I am not morally obliged to continue experiencing a pleasure I am now experiencing, even though it may have value, and even though by ceasing to experience it I thereby end its existence. Likewise, from the mere fact (assuming it is a fact) that conscious awareness in itself has value, it does not follow that suicide (which presumably brings one's conscious awareness to an end) is always morally wrong. Just as I am morally allowed to abandon an instance of pleasure, even though it has some value, I may be morally allowed to terminate my conscious awareness, even though it has value.

According to the view developed here, the permissibility of a particular act of suicide depends on whether or not it involves violating a duty or set of duties to another person or group which overrides the rights that would otherwise justify suicide. Were it not for duties to others, all suicide would be permissible. Determining whether a particular suicide which violates duties to others is morally permissible or not is a matter of weighing the derived right to commit suicide against duties to others.

Unfortunately, it can be extremely difficult in practice to weigh rights against duties. Clearly, if one were to demand a criterion which would easily determine the moral status of every possible case of suicide, our account would not satisfy such a demand. However, any criterion that would make it a very simple matter to decide whether any particular case of suicide is permissible or not would be suspicious since it is, in fact, frequently very difficult to reach a justified moral judgment on suicide; any criterion that would easily determine the moral status of every suicide would have to be arbitrary; it would have to be imposed on our moral beliefs rather than derived from them.

Until we discuss obligatory suicide, we will ignore cases in which other-regarding considerations exist that actually *favor* suicide. Here we have in mind what can be called "self-regarding suicide," suicide which is not favored by any other-regarding considerations whatsoever. The point of focusing on self-regarding suicide is that doing so will allow us to consider the rights and circumstances that justify suicide in the face of duties to others that would be violated by suicide. Other-regarding factors that might actually increase the weight of the right to suicide will be discussed in the next section, where we will consider the issue of obligatory suicide.

The most basic case of self-regarding suicide occurs when an individual simply has no duties to others at all. On our view, duties to others constitute the sole limitation of the permissibility of suicide; were it not for such duties, all suicide would be permissible. The permissibility of suicide in cases where the individual has absolutely no duties to others derives from the right to act as one sees fit; if one simply has no duties to others, his right to act as he chooses is not limited in any way. Consequently, he is morally permitted to commit suicide. Naturally, this does not commit us to the claim that all suicides which occur in the absence of duties to others are *praiseworthy*. It might, for example, be more praiseworthy to increase one's knowledge or create objects of beauty. The issue of whether or not the agent of an act deserves praise for the act is distinct from the issue of whether or not the act is morally permissible; morally permissible acts can be performed on the basis of unpraiseworthy motives.

However, since at least virtually everyone has duties to others, the rest of this section will be devoted to considering the kinds of rights and circumstances that justify self-regarding suicide in the face of duties to others that would be violated by that act; that is, in the rest of this section we will have in mind suicides in which the agent does have duties to others, and where none of these duties actually favors suicide, while at least some would be violated by suicide. Once we focus on self-regarding suicide in the face of duties to others that would be violated by suicide, we have to consider the kinds of rights and circumstances that allow for the moral permissibility of such suicide; that is, what factors can increase the weight of the rights which justify suicide to the point where they are not overridden by the agent's duties to others?

By far the most important circumstance that may justify suicide is personal suffering of various sorts. We saw earlier that our account does not have the implication that the suicides of persons with identical duties to others must also have the same moral status. The explanation for this was that other factors may strengthen one's right to commit suicide, and if any such factor is present in one case of suicide and absent in another, the two suicides might differ in moral status; one might be permissible while the other is impermissible. One such factor is pain, especially intense, enduring, and unremediable pain. Let us call such pain "profound pain."

The presence of profound pain may increase the weight of the right to commit suicide. Depending on how profound the pain is (i.e., how intense, enduring, or unremediable), the weight of this right might surpass that of one's duties to others. In such a case, one's right to commit suicide has not been overridden and suicide would be morally permissible. This explains by means of one kind of example how suicide can be permissible in one case but impermissible in another even though the two persons involved have identical duties to others; profound pain may be so profound that it tips the scale in favor of the right to suicide.

We will have to include not only "physical pain," but also so-called "mental pain." I will not attempt to show that this popular distinction survives criticism since whether it does or not will not affect our claim. Profound "mental pain" (if such a thing exists) may also justify suicide.

If we use "suffering" to cover every kind of physical or mental pain, I think we can see that it is usually *actual* or *potential* suffering which increases the weight of one's right to commit suicide in the face of duties to others. Most other reasons which might be given to defend one's right to commit suicide seem to reduce to suffering. For instance, if it is claimed that public humiliation may increase the weight of the right to commit suicide, it seems clear that what increases the weight of the right to commit suicide is not simply the objective fact of public ridicule, but the personal suffering involved. Likewise, if it is claimed that being reduced to poverty is a condition that may increase the weight of one's right to commit suicide, it seems that it is not simply the amount of money one has relative to others that counts; rather, it is the suffering involved in being reduced to poverty. (If poverty involves degradation, then, as we shall see, this may also increase the weight of the right to commit suicide.)

As noted above, we must include potential suffering, as well as actual suffering, as a consideration that may increase the weight of one's right to commit suicide. For example, the prospect of an intensely painful terminal illness may increase the weight of one's right to commit suicide, even though one is not now suffering any pain or even showing any obvious signs of illness. In cases like this, we are considering the relevance of potential suffering to the moral status of suicide.

While suffering is the most notable type of phenomenon that may strengthen one's right to commit suicide, and clearly the one most often mentioned, there are also properties of this suffering that affect the strength of the right to commit suicide in the face of contrary duties to others. The properties I have in mind are those mentioned by Jeremy Bentham in his discussion of the measurement of the value of pleasure and pain.[14] First, quantitative properties have to be considered. Here we have in mind such features as intensity and duration. The more intense the suffering in question, or the more enduring, the more weight may need to be added to the right to commit suicide. Second, the certainty or uncertainty of the suffering must also be considered. The more certain the suffering, the more likely we are to increase the weight of the right to commit suicide. An analogous point applies to the nearness or remoteness of the suffering; one's right to commit suicide now is not strengthened much (if at all) by the prospect, certain though it may be, of suffering in the very distant future. Bentham also mentions relational properties that are relevant; how the suffering is or will be related to other factors that may affect the right to commit suicide must be considered. For example, if the original instance of suffering will produce other instances, this may affect the strength of one's right to commit suicide. (Bentham also mentions the extent of pain, by which he means the number of persons affected by it. This feature will have to be discussed in the next section in relation to the issue of obligatory suicide.)

The reason why suffering can affect the weight of the right to commit suicide is that suicide can, for obvious reasons, be an effective method of ending suffering by merely eliminating the sufferer. We are quite willing to say that persons in certain situations involving personal suffering are morally permitted to act in ways that would otherwise be morally wrong. For example, one is morally permitted to break a small promise if fulfilling it would cause one a great deal of pain. Suppose that Jones has promised to play the violin at his sister's birthday party, but since he made that promise he has undergone a hand operation, as a result of which playing the violin would cause him intense pain. Assuming that these are the only relevant facts of the case, Jones is permitted to break his promise. On the other hand, if Jones would suffer only very slight discomfort, he may not be permitted to break his promise.

In this example, we have focused on the intensity of the pain to make our point. However, it is easy to construct examples using other features of suffering discussed above to show that variations in these features can affect the moral permissibility of actions and to establish the main point that the presence or absence of suffering of certain sorts plays a major role in determining the moral status of suicide. On the view presented here, suffering of various sorts can play a major role in the weight of one's right to commit suicide and can allow this right to override the suicide's duties to others, in which case suicide is morally permissible.

If we ask what makes suffering of all sorts relevant to the question of the weight of the right to commit suicide, the answer seems to be that the appearance of personal suffering is the most obvious instance of a decrease in the potential suicide's personal well-being. (Of course, suffering might be causally required for an increase in overall personal well-being, but, considered in itself, the appearance of suffering always constitutes a decrease in personal well-being.) This would suggest that perhaps other kinds of decrease in personal well-being are relevant as well. Or is pain of various sorts the only kind of phenomenon that negatively affects one's well-being?

Unless one were to measure well-being simply in terms of pleasure and pain, one would have to consider other kinds of decrease in personal well-being. I reject the claim that personal well-being is simply a function of the amount of pleasure and pain one's life contains because it seems that other factors affect well-being independently of the pleasure and pain they involve. For example, whether or not one is profoundly insane seems to affect one's well-being independently of whatever pleasure or pain is involved. For those who think that personal well-being is simply a function of pleasure and pain, the issue of suicide will be that much easier to handle, but for those who agree that other elements are relevant to well-being, these other elements will have to be considered in forming a judgment on the moral status of a case of suicide.

Naturally, it would be impossible in the present work to discuss all the sorts of things the presence or absence of which might plausibly be thought to affect personal well-being; that would form a volume in itself, and, given the predictably diverse opinions of philosophers, a lengthy and controversial one. But I will mention what I think is the most important factor for our discussion other than pain of various sorts: degrading conditions.

Degrading conditions, considered in themselves, seem to constitute a serious blow to one's well-being independently of the pain they may happen to involve. The life of the slave who enjoys all sorts of pleasure may not be as good as that of the free person who enjoys less pleasure. Degrading medical procedures which are administered in order to sustain life are even more relevant to our concern. One can plausibly claim that such degrading procedures reduce the well-being of the patient independently of whatever suffering he might feel; he may, in fact, feel none. We should also mention cases in which individuals are forced to live in ways that violate their deepest moral convictions. Being forced to act contrary to one's deepest moral convictions is a form of degradation that constitutes a serious blow to one's well-being. This category would include those persons who were forced to participate in genocide and torture by their Nazi oppressors.

What we said about the characteristics of suffering also applies in the case of degradation. Not only must potential degradation be considered; but such factors as the intensity and duration of the degradation are relevant. The same can be said for the nearness or remoteness of it, the certainty or uncertainty of it, and its relations to other factors that affect personal well-being. If, for example, a certain intensity of degradation increases the weight of one's right to commit suicide, a more intense degradation will increase it even more, assuming all other factors are held constant.

Suicide in cases in which the individual in question has no duties to others whatsoever can be justified merely by appealing to one's prima facie right to act as one sees fit; duties to others which would limit this right are not present in such cases. When one has no duties to others whatsoever, one's right of self-determination is sufficient to establish the moral permissibility of one's suicide, however prudentially irrational or unpraiseworthy such an act of suicide may be. In cases in which one does have duties to others, and in which none of those duties favors suicide, while at least some count against suicide, circumstances which negatively affect one's well-being may justify suicide. In this kind of case we have to consider not only the general right to act as one sees fit (i.e., one's right of self-determination); in cases of this sort involving circumstances that negatively affect one's well-being, we must take into account the more specific right to maximize one's well-being, which includes the right to escape from circumstances which negatively affect one's well-being.

However, with respect to these kinds of cases, we must add the very important cautionary note that it is easy to assume that the right to maximize one's well-being justifies suicide when in fact it merely justifies another act. If, for instance, I am considering suicide as a means of escaping personal suffering, and if I have duties to others that would be violated by my suicide, then the suffering, no matter how horrible, will not justify suicide if I could just as easily escape it with a medication that would allow me to fulfill most of my duties to others. Likewise, even if I face the prospect of extreme degradation, I am not permitted to commit suicide if some other action would easily allow me to avoid the degradation while also allowing me to violate fewer duties to others.

What these and other possible examples show is that, when considering the permissibility of self-regarding suicide to avoid circumstances that negatively affect one's well-being, we must consider alternatives to suicide and compare them to suicide in terms of the agent's well-being and his duties to others. That is, we have to consider (i) the agent's right to maximize his well-being (which includes the right to avoid conditions which negatively affect an individual's well-being), (ii) his set of duties to others, and (iii) the available options. Then, with the available options in mind, we must try to find the best way of doing justice to the agent's right to maximize his well-being while doing justice to his duties to others. If one's well-being would be equally served by two acts, and if one act involves violating duties to others while the other does not, clearly the simple appeal to one's right to maximize one's well-being will not justify acting in the way that involves a violation of duty. The difficult cases arise when we face various options with different consequences in terms of both personal well-being and duties to others. If, for example, one act would best maximize my well-being, while another would serve my interests to a slightly lesser extent but would involve me in a slightly less extreme violation of duties to others, it may be unclear how I should choose between these. Unfortunately, there is no formula that would enable us to determine the morally correct course of action in such circumstances; there is no formula that enables us to weigh the right to maximize one's well-being against duties to others. Many cases, of course, seem easy, but one could always devise examples in which it is unclear whether the agent's right to maximize his well-being overrides his duties to others.

So far we have considered the very general right to act as one sees fit; the more specific right to maximize one's well-being; and the right to avoid circumstances that negatively affect one's well-being, the latter right being a species of the right to maximize one's well-being. All were shown to justify suicide in certain kinds of circumstances. It seems that these are the most important rights to consider with respect to self-regarding suicide since personal suffering is such a widespread reason for suicide.

However, there may be cases in which other rights might justify self-regarding suicide. For example, some authors have defended "symbolic protest" suicide.[15] Suppose that committing suicide in a certain manner is an effective method of expressing one's deepest values. One might, for instance, intend to die by starvation as a statement of protest against the government's failure to help the hungry. To use a more familiar example, suicide by self-immolation might be a way of expressing one's contempt for existing political circumstances.[16] The right to express one's deepest values might justify self-regarding suicide. Such suicides might be permissible even if we ignore other-regarding factors that might favor them.[17] To determine the moral status of such suicides, we will have to take into account the duties to others that would be violated by suicide, the alternative ways of expressing the same thought, and the individual's right to express her deepest values. It may be that the individual has no strong duties to others that would be violated by his suicide, and that suicide is the best means of expressing his deepest values; because of government repression, for example, none of the usual ways of expressing discontent may be available. In such a case, self-regarding suicide seems permissible, depending on the weakness of the agent's duties to others.

We can conclude this section by noting that, although we have said that duties to others limit the permissibility of suicide, the state of affairs in which one's duties to others would render one's suicide morally impermissible can be fleeting. So far we have ignored the fact that many such duties can be fulfilled before one commits suicide. So even though one's suicide may be wrong given one's existing duties, the moral status of the act could change if one were to reduce the overall weight of one's duties to others by fulfilling those that could be fulfilled prior to suicide. If, for example, the only duty which overrides my right to commit suicide is an important promise, it may be possible to fulfill this promise prior to committing suicide. So although suicide may be ruled out because of overriding duties to others, this situation can be quite fleeting if one can modify the weight of one's duties to others by fulfilling at least some of them prior to suicide.

Obligatory Suicide

So far, we have concerned ourselves with self-regarding suicide, suicide in which there are no other-regarding factors at all that favor suicide, and our main concern has been with a species of self-regarding suicide: those that involve the violation of a duty or set of duties to others. When we turn to other-regarding factors that actually favor suicide, we face the question: is one ever morally required to commit suicide? (Other-regarding factors that contribute to the permissibility of suicide without making it obligatory can be discussed in connection with this question since all obligatory suicide is permissible and since the factors that make suicide obligatory may make it merely permissible when they are present in weaker form.)

At first sight, it seems easy to think of a case in which suicide is obligatory. Consider the following scenario. Jones discovers that he has an extremely rare and incurable mental illness that will shortly lead him commit horrendous acts of murder unless he is somehow prevented from doing so. However, he knows that others are unwilling to detain him in a jail cell or mental institution; they simply do not believe that he has the illness in question. After all, he once made a similar claim in the past and proved to be mistaken. Further, Jones knows that he cannot prevent himself from committing the murders by, say, locking himself in his house; his house will not contain him when he slips into madness. Nor can Jones prevent himself from harming others by becoming a hermit in the wilderness; once insane, he will inevitably find his way back to civilization. In short, we can stipulate that the only way Jones can guarantee that others are spared his murderous rampage is to cease living.[18]

One might also imagine a case in which a General--Smith-- will bring destruction upon his troops by remaining alive. Smith has been captured by an enemy who has a drug which will cause him to reveal information that would cost the lives of thousands of his troops. The only way for Smith to avoid the massacre of his troops is to commit suicide.

Those who are not convinced that all suicide is wrong might be inclined to say that cases like those just described are cases in which a person is obliged to commit suicide. As we have seen, however, some philosophers have worried that certain positions commit their proponents to the disturbing conclusion that many more people are obliged to commit suicide than we might otherwise have thought. After all, if one accepts a utilitarian position, it might easily be the case that suicide would bring about a greater balance of happiness over unhappiness than any other option. Further, as we saw earlier, Battin finds it disturbing that a theory like ours regarding the permissibility of suicide suggests the view that other-regarding considerations might make suicide obligatory in certain cases. Others have flatly stated that any view which leads to the conclusion that suicide can be obligatory is thereby self-evidently false. The notion that suicide can be obligatory, then, is a notion which some find both disturbing and implausible, if not self-evidently false.

Nevertheless, I think we are going to have to admit the existence of cases of obligatory suicide. The reason is that other-regarding considerations seem to require suicide in certain kinds of cases. I submit that the examples discussed above concerning Jones (the would-be murderous psychopath) and General Smith are clear cases where, because of the seriousness of the cost to others, suicide is not only morally permitted but required.

What is strange is that this conclusion is seen as utterly implausible. After all, even Plato, who is sometimes mistakenly regarded as endorsing a general prohibition of suicide, claims that suicide may sometimes be obligatory. In considering the case of a deranged temple robber, he imagines commanding such a person to take action to free himself from his malady: "And if it be so that by thus acting your disease grows less, well; but if not, deem death the more noble way, and quit yourself of life."[19] Further, we are quite willing to demand great sacrifices from individuals in other cases. During what is perceived to be a just war, people may be expected to risk their jobs, their happiness, their security, their health, and even their lives to protect others from occupation by foreign armies. Admittedly, during a war we usually ask only that people place their lives at great risk, which is quite different from requiring death. However, we would ask people to kill themselves before providing the Gestapo with information of various kinds (e.g., information concerning the manufacture of the atomic bomb). Further, since we know that some people will be killed in any war, we think of the right to life as being overrideable by duties to others. The right to life is not "absolute" but "prima facie"; it is overrideable. If self-sacrifices of other kinds are morally required on some occasions, what is so implausible about the claim that self-sacrificial suicide can be morally required on some occasions?

What disturbs Battin is that people who are burdens to others might be looked upon as being obliged to kill themselves. Consider Nietzsche's reflections on the ill, reflections which were not applied by his own doctors:

> The sick man is a parasite of society. In a certain state it is indecent to live longer. To go on vegetating in cowardly dependence on physicians and machinations, after the meaning of life, the right to life, has been lost, that ought to prompt a profound contempt in society. The physicians, in turn, would have to be the mediators of this contempt--not prescriptions, but every day a new dose of nausea with their patients.[20]

Battin refers to this passage in an attempt to cast doubt on the idea of obligatory suicide.[21] The desired conclusion is that the idea of obligatory suicide is incompatible with powerful moral intuitions that most people have concerning the sick.

Clearly, if we were to accept the view that anyone who is in any way a burden to others is obliged to commit suicide, we would run against strong moral convictions. But I am not proposing such a view. To say that other-regarding considerations may make suicide obligatory is not to say that any inconvenience to others caused by one's continued existence results in an obligation to kill oneself. We have to weigh the individual's right to continue living against his duties to others. The right to continue living is not overridden the instant others are in any way inconvenienced by one's continued existence, just as the right to commit suicide is not overridden the instant others would be at all inconvenienced by one's suicide.

When, then, is suicide morally required? The abstract answer is that it is required when one's continued life would involve one in the violation of duties to others which override one's rights, especially one's right to life. To bring this principle closer to earth, we have to consider some of the kinds of situations in which this occurs.

What the examples above show is not only that the deaths of others are relevant; they also show that suffering on the part of others that inevitably arises as a result of one's continued life may override one's right to life, in which case suicide will be obligatory. Of course, all the factors that were mentioned with regard to personal suffering in the last section (i.e., intensity, duration, etc.) will also have to be considered, plus one more: the extent of the suffering, or how many people it affects. To consider the actual or potential suffering of others as a possible source of a duty to commit suicide mirrors other moral convictions we hold with respect to other kinds of personal sacrifice. To revert to our previous example, in the case of a just war one may be obliged to make great personal sacrifices in order to avoid enormous harm to others.

However, it would be a mistake to ignore the fact that the right to continue living is extremely strong; it is not immediately overridden by the fact that other lives could be saved if one were to kill oneself. For example, one is not obliged to kill oneself so that a few persons in desperate need of organ transplants might be spared early deaths and a great deal of suffering. Even if one's death were a necessary condition for the continued existence of a few other victims of organ failure, one is not obliged to kill oneself. It even seems to be the case that if one's death were a necessary condition for the full recovery of a few victims of organ failure, one would still not be morally required to sacrifice one's life. Killing oneself in such a situation may be praised as heroic, but it would be seen as above and beyond the call of duty.

On the other hand, it does seem to be the case that the suffering of others can in certain kinds of cases override one's right to life. If, for example, my refraining from self-destruction would bring about unendurable agony for thousands, it seems hard to deny that I am obliged to commit suicide. So while we have to admit that the suffering of others can give rise to a duty to commit suicide, the weight of one's right to continue living makes it very difficult for such suffering to create an obligation to kill oneself. The obligation to commit suicide is not an obligation that many of us will ever face.

Just as degrading circumstances were relevant to the issue of permissible suicide independently of the personal suffering involved, an analogous claim seems to be true in the case of obligatory suicide. If one's continued existence would create degrading circumstances for others (e.g., slavery), one may be obliged to kill oneself, depending, of course, on the intensity and duration of the degradation, its certainty, its nearness, its relations to other relevant factors (e.g., other instances of degradation or suffering), and its extent. It is not the case that any instance of actual or potential degradation on the part of others brought about by one's continued existence will give rise to an obligation to commit suicide.

Other duties beside the duty to prevent unwanted suffering and degradation may also have to be considered. For instance, some may argue that if there is a duty to make others happy beyond what is involved in the mere elimination or reduction of their suffering and degradation, then suicide may be required, depending, as always, on the weight of this duty and the weight of the right to continue living. However, it seems to me that even if we admit the existence of a duty to promote happiness beyond what is involved in eliminating or reducing unhappiness--and it is not at all clear that we should admit that this duty exists--such a duty would never be weighty enough to require suicide. It seems very implausible to suggest that I am obliged to commit suicide because by doing so I will make a relatively happy population even happier.

The same factors that make suicide obligatory in certain cases would make suicide merely permissible (i.e., permissible but not obligatory) in cases in which those factors are mitigated. If, for example, one is obliged to kill oneself to avoid the degradation of millions, then one's suicide could be permissible, though not obligatory, if substantially less degradation were involved. Likewise, if one's continued existence constitutes such an extreme burden to society that suicide is obligatory, then the fact that one's continued existence constitutes less of a burden may justify suicide even though it would not make suicide obligatory. Other-regarding factors, then, may make suicide permissible even when they fail to make it obligatory.

Conclusion

Suicide may be justified by appealing to the suicide's (or would-be suicide's) rights. We discussed suicide in relation to the right to act as one sees fit, the right to maximize one's well-being, and the right to escape circumstances that negatively affect one's well-being (a species of the last right). We also noted that other rights might justify suicide in certain circumstances. As an example, we focused on the right to express one's deepest values (which might also be construed as part of the right to maximize one's well-being). If one had no duties to others, the permissibility of suicide would stem from the right to act as one sees fit; one's self-determination right would suffice to render one's suicide morally permissible, even though suicide in the circumstances may be prudentially irrational in the extreme, and even though one's motives for committing suicide may merit no praise. Where one does have duties to others, we have to weigh those duties against the various rights that might justify suicide. If the duties do not outweigh the rights, suicide is permissible.

Duties to others not only limit the permissibility of suicide; sometimes they justify it, and sometimes they make it obligatory. We saw that suicide may be obligatory in circumstances where, for example, the well-being of others is seriously negatively affected by one's continued existence. The factors affecting well-being that seemed most important were suffering, degrading circumstances, and deaths (if sufficient numbers are at stake). Here again we have to weigh rights against duties, the suicide's right to continue living against his duties to others. We also mentioned the controversial duty to make others happy beyond what is involved in freeing them from suffering and degradation as a possible source of obligatory suicide; if there really is such a duty (which is questionable), some might claim that it may give rise to an obligation to kill oneself. However, given the weight of one's right to continue living, it seems to me quite implausible to suggest that such a duty could be weighty enough to make suicide obligatory.

It would be nice to be able to conclude with a neat formula that would allow us to determine with mechanical ease the moral status of every imaginable case of suicide, given that we knew all the non-moral facts of any case at hand. It would be nice to be able to serve up a principle that would allow us to determine whether or not a given suicide is permissible and whether or not it is obligatory as well as permissible. Unfortunately, I cannot do so. The reason is that there is no precise way to measure the relative strengths of rights and duties to others. It is not simply that there is no instrument that would make such a measurement possible; rather, our moral convictions are not precise enough to allow us to give exact and non-arbitrary comparisons of the strengths of the rights and duties in question. One could, of course, insist that there must be a precise principle which could allow us to answer with certainty our questions concerning the moral status of every particular case of suicide. Further, there are principles available that satisfy the demand for precision. For example, one might adopt the principle that suicide is permissible if and only if it does not cause anyone other than the suicide any sensations of pain. Or one might adopt the principle that suicide is permissible if and only if no other act available to the agent has a higher utility. Or simpler still, one might adopt the principle that all suicide is permissible or the principle that all suicide is impermissible. However, such principles, however precise they may be, are implausible for various reasons. There may indeed be a principle which satisfies the demand for precision and easy application and which coheres with strong moral beliefs people have or which can be justified without appealing to commonly accepted moral convictions. However, intellectual honesty would force most philosophers to admit that centuries of philosophy have proved insufficient to produce such a principle. Until a true general criterion of moral permissibility is established (assuming such an event is even possible), we are forced to try as best we can to evaluate actions without one. I have tried in this chapter to point to general considerations which bear on the moral status of individual cases of suicide. Our view does point out common factors that have to be considered in determining the moral status of suicide. Further, our discussion has shown that what we must do to determine the moral status of suicide is make our judgment concerning a particular suicide square with our deepest convictions about analogous actions. For example, we can sometimes compare suicide to emigration. When this can be done, we should try to make our judgment about suicide square with our judgment concerning emigration. Suicide can sometimes be compared to abandonment. In such cases, we should try to make our judgment about the suicide in question mirror our judgment about abandonment in the same circumstances. In judging the moral status of particular cases of suicide, we must rely on analogies to other actions and consider our moral convictions about the latter. The goal is to make our judgments about suicide square with our deepest moral convictions.

We have thrown light on the issues involved in determining the moral status of suicide, but, unfortunately, no handy formula is available to make this task easy. It is an inherently difficult task, and perhaps what we have thrown the most light on is the reason why suicide is such a difficult moral issue.

Notes

1. Margaret P. Battin, *Ethical Issues in Suicide* (Englewood Cliffs: Prentice-Hall, 1982), 182.

2. Ibid.

3. Margaret P. Battin, "Suicide: A Fundamental Human Right?," in *Suicide: The Philosophical Issues*, ed. M.P. Battin and D.J. Mayo (London: Peter Owen, 1980), 268. The teenager's suicide is an actual case.

4. Battin, *Ethical Issues in Suicide*, 183.

5. The suicide/emigration analogy derives from Thomas Szasz, "The Ethics of Suicide," in *Suicide: The Philosophical Issues*, ed. M.P. Battin and D.J. Mayo, 196.

6. Battin, "Suicide: A Fundamental Human Right?," 270.

7. Ibid.

8. J.P. Moreland and Norman L. Geisler, *The Life and Death Debate* (Westport: Greenwood Press, 1990), 94.

9. Paul-Louis Landsberg, *The Moral Problem of Suicide*, trans. C. Rowland (New York: Philosophical Library, 1953), 84.

Battin endorses this passage in "Suicide: A Fundamental Human Right?," 282.

10. Seneca, "The Stoic View," in *Suicide: Right or Wrong?*, ed. John Donnelly (Buffalo: Prometheus Books, 1990), 29.

11. Eliot Slater, "Choosing the Time to Die," in *Suicide: The Philosophical Issues*, ed. M.P. Battin and D.J. Mayo, 202.

12. Eike-Henner W. Kluge, *The Practice of Death* (New Haven: Yale University Press, 1975), 119.

13. Battin, *Ethical Issues in Suicide*, 180.

14. Jeremy Bentham, *An Introduction to the Principles of Morals and Legislation*, in *The English Philosophers from Bacon to Mill*, ed. Edwin. A. Burtt (New York: Modern Library, 1939), 803.

15. Karen Lebacqz and H. Tristram Engelhardt, "Suicide," in *Death, Dying, and Euthanasia*, ed. Dennis Horan and David Mall (Frederick: Aletheia Books, 1980), 691. After attacking anti-suicide arguments, these authors present an extremely sketchy treatment (scarcely over three pages) of permissible suicide which is similar to our position on permissible suicide. However, they focus entirely on duties of "covenant-fidelity."

16. See David Wood, "Suicide as Instrument and Expression," in *Suicide: The Philosophical Issues*, ed. M.P. Battin and D.J. Mayo, 154-55.

17. Lebacqz and Engelhardt defend symbolic protest suicide on other-regarding grounds in their "Suicide," 692-93.

18. This example derives from R.F. Holland, *Against Empiricism* (Oxford: Basil Blackwell, 1980), 149-50.

19. Plato, *Laws*, trans. R.G. Bury (Cambridge: Harvard University Press, 1967), 854c.

20. Friedrich Nietzsche, *The Portable Nietzsche*, ed. and trans. Walter Kaufmann (New York: Viking, 1954), 536.

21. Battin, *Ethical Issues in Suicide*, 99.

CHAPTER 4

THE ROLE OF OTHERS IN SUICIDE

The questions to be discussed in this chapter include the following: what role should others play in suicide? Should they attempt to prevent all suicide? Or are others obliged to prevent only some suicides? Are preventive measures ever even permissible? If preventive measures are not always called for, are there cases in which others should actually assist the would-be suicide in killing himself? If so, how can abuses be prevented?

Authors from various disciplines have brought forth reasons for preventing all, or at least virtually all, suicide. We will consider these arguments in an attempt to determine whether or not, and in what circumstances, others should prevent a suicide from realizing his intentions. Once again, we shall reach a moderate conclusion: some suicide may legitimately be prevented, but not all. Arguments for the view that all suicide should be prevented are unacceptable.

After dealing with the prevention issue, we will consider the assistance issue: are there cases in which others should facilitate suicide? As we shall see, there are cases in which one is obliged to facilitate suicide. However, personal sacrifices of various sorts may make suicide assistance non-obligatory.

Preventing Suicide

I will assume that totally uncoercive suicide prevention measures need no justification. For example, merely presenting the would-be suicide with one's anti-suicide position requires no justification. Suggesting a psychotherapist for the person who seeks relief from his suicidal impulses also requires no justification. For the remainder of this section I will have in mind coercive preventive measures (e.g., involuntary hospitalization, medication, etc.).

One finds in the literature on suicide several claims which are thought to justify the coercive prevention of all, or at least almost all, suicide. These arguments can be grouped into three categories: psychological arguments, epistemological arguments, and ethical arguments. All attempt to establish a conclusion concerning the ethical status of coercive suicide prevention, but the first two categories are distinguished by the fact that they appeal to special claims about the psychology of suicide or about the bounds of human knowledge. I will first consider psychological claims which are thought to justify preventive measures with respect to suicide in all, or at least virtually all, cases. Epistemological and ethical arguments for coercive suicide prevention will then be considered.

Psychological Arguments

Mental Illness: By far the most important psychological argument with respect to suicide prevention is the claim that suicide prevention is justified since suicide is always or at least virtually always a manifestation of some form of mental illness. We are told that the suicidal option is almost always chosen under "pathological circumstances or under the influence of diseased feelings."[1] Further, so-called "rational" suicide is a rarity since most persons who commit suicide are "suffering from clinically recognizable psychiatric illnesses often carrying an excellent prognosis."[2] From this some are led to infer that the therapist must not only make clear to the patient that he "believes such behavior arises from the patient's illness"; he must "do everything he can to prevent it, enlisting the rest of the staff in this effort." Further, the claim is made that suicidal intent "must not be part of therapeutic confidentiality in a hospital setting."[3]

However, as we briefly noted in Chapter 1, there is a great deal of disagreement on the relation between suicide and mental illness. First, even some of those who accept the claim that perhaps most of those who attempt suicide are "limited in their ability to think and act rationally by some mental illness" admit that "it would be extremely difficult" to justify the claim that all suicide attempts are products of mental illness.[4] Further, psychiatrist Thomas Szasz claims that the view that suicide is a manifestation of mental illness is "both erroneous and evil": erroneous since "it treats an act as if it were a happening"; and evil because it "serves to legitimize psychiatric force and fraud by justifying it as medical care and treatment."[5] Finally, some psychiatrists take a moderate view, regarding many suicides as mentally ill, while allowing that many make realistic estimations of their options.[6] It is therefore not surprising that after examining the psychiatric material pertaining to suicide, Margaret Battin reaches the following conclusion: "There is clearly no consensus on the frequency of mental illness in suicide or suicide attempts"; in fact, estimates of the percentage of mentally ill among suicides have ranged from as low as 20% to as high as 100%.[7] However, one point on which there is widespread agreement is that relatively few suicides are psychotic.[8] (It would be ironic if most suicides were psychotic since, on some estimates, the suicide rate for psychiatrists is almost seven times that of the general population.[9])

Even if we accept the claim that the desire to commit suicide is a manifestation of some form of mental illness, that *in itself* would not justify preventive measures. The desire to produce a comprehensive metaphysical system might be (and no doubt has been) a manifestation of mental illness, but that in itself would not justify others in preventing its realization. Even the desire to recover from one's mental illness might be a by-product of the illness, but surely no one would suggest that this justifies perpetuating the patient's illness. So even if one could show that all suicidal desires are products of mental illness (which is clearly not the case), that alone would not justify preventive measures.

Although these examples show that the fact that a desire arises from mental illness is not *in itself* sufficient to justify the coercive prevention of its realization, one might claim that the self-harming aspect of suicide, when combined with the presence of mental illness, justifies the coercive prevention of suicide. However, even this claim is false, for we do not always consider it appropriate to prevent those with mental illnesses from realizing their desires, even when those desires are related to their illnesses and their fulfillment would cause the agent harm. For example, even if we discovered that a person's religious practices (e.g., fasting) were due in part to some minor neurosis, we would not (other-regarding factors aside) consider it appropriate to prevent the person from engaging in these practices, even if such practices were harmful to the agent.[10] However, more will be said about the appeal to mental illness below.

The Cry for Help Model of Attempted Suicide: A second psychological thesis that is used to justify coercive suicide prevention measures asserts that potential suicides wish to be saved; suicidal behavior is a "cry for help." Suicidologist Edwin Shneidman is the main proponent of this view: "Individuals who are intent on killing themselves still wish very much to be rescued or to have their deaths prevented." Consequently, suicide prevention consists essentially in recognizing that the potential suicide is ambivalent between his wishes to live and his wishes to die, then "throwing one's efforts on the side of life."[11]

This attempt to justify coercive suicide prevention measures is problematic. In support of this view, one might appeal to the fact that a high percentage of would-be suicides appreciate being saved. However, this would only provide a limited defense since some survivors express bitterness over their "rescue."[12] Further, it is doubtful that those who attempt to commit suicide in ways that make it easy for others to save them fall into the same class as those who attempt suicide in ways which make it nearly impossible for others to save them. The claim that someone who committed suicide by firing a shotgun into his mouth was communicating a desperate "cry for help" seems quite implausible; it is unlikely that those who want to be rescued would make it virtually impossible for others to rescue them.

However, there is an even more serious problem with the cry for help justification of coercive suicide prevention measures. Shneidman's view is that potential suicides have serious doubts about suicide even though they also have pro-attitudes toward suicide. However, this in itself does not justify suicide prevention. Whenever one makes a difficult choice, it is likely that one will still have doubts, but this in itself does not show that others are justified in preventing us from carrying out our decisions.[13] When somebody makes a career choice, he may have serious doubts about the wisdom of his choice, but such doubts do not allow others to prevent him from carrying out his choice. More will be said about the appeal to ambivalence below, after we discuss a third psychological argument for suicide prevention.

The Transitoriness of the Suicidal Desire: A third psychological thesis, which is repeated quite frequently in the literature, claims that the wish to die by suicide is usually fleeting: "The desire to terminate one's life is usually transient. The 'right' to suicide is a 'right' desired only temporarily." From this a momentous conclusion is immediately reached: "Every physician should feel the obligation to support the desire for life."[14]

Here again it would be a mistake to use an invalid argument of the following form: since most potential suicides have a certain characteristic, this in itself justifies treating all potential suicides as if they had that characteristic. Even if the desire for suicide is transient in most cases, that in itself will not justify the claim that all suicide should be prevented. One can easily imagine cases in which individuals think long and hard on the suicidal option before embracing it.

Further, why should the simple fact that a desire is transient justify others in preventing its realization? The desire to do something very good for others might be fleeting, but that in itself does not show that others are justified in preventing its realization. Clearly, the lifespan of a desire does not *in itself* determine whether or not one should prevent its realization, otherwise one would have to say that a transitory desire to do good for others must be frustrated.

The appeal to the claim that *most* suicide results from mental illness, the appeal to the alleged ambivalence of *most* suicides, and the appeal to the alleged transitoriness of *most* suicidal impulses all fail to justify the claim that *all* suicide should be prevented. Further, since the mere fact that a desire springs from mental illness, the mere fact that one is ambivalent about it, and the mere fact it is fleeting are each insufficient to show that the desire's realization should be prevented, it turns out that appealing to mental illness, ambivalence, or to the fleeting nature of suicidal impulses will not *in itself* justify suicide prevention *in any case whatsoever*. Further, even if one made an appeal to all three claims (i.e., the mental illness claim, the ambivalence claim, and the transitoriness claim), it seems that that in itself would not justify any preventive measures. Why, then, have so many authors repeatedly appealed to these alleged facts in an attempt to justify coercive suicide prevention measures?

With respect to the mental illness claim, the reason may be that mental illness is related to something else which is relevant to the question of suicide prevention: the potential suicide's factual (non-moral) beliefs. Whether or not someone has correct factual beliefs is relevant to the issue of paternalistic interference. If, for example, laymen want to take certain drugs in the belief that they will be cured of their ailments, when in fact they would be seriously harmed, laws which attempt to prevent them from obtaining the drugs without prescriptions may be justified.[15] Mental illness enters the picture when we realize the impact it can have on one's factual beliefs; depending on the severity of the illness, one might come to hold ludicrous factual beliefs. For example, one might come to believe the following: "Unless I kill myself, I'll become a werewolf." In cases where mental illness creates factual ignorance which gives rise to suicidal intentions, suicide prevention may be justified. Even in such a case, it would be inaccurate to say that the presence of mental illness justifies preventive measures; the factual errors justify preventive measures; the mental illness simply happens in this case to be responsible for the factual ignorance which is partially responsible for the desire to commit suicide.

Mental illness is also relevant when it prevents someone from acting on his deepest desires, even though it may not involve factual ignorance. One might, for example, be the victim of irrational fears or compulsions which push one toward self-destruction, even though one may also have a rationally formed desire to live. In such cases, preventive measures seem justified. (It should be noted, however, that, given the analysis of suicide presented in the appendix, it is unclear that self-destruction due to compulsions counts as suicide.)

As for the appeals to ambivalence (the cry for help model) and the alleged transitoriness of suicidal desires, these claims seem relevant to factual beliefs about one's deepest desires; if one is ambivalent, one may say, "I don't know what I want," and transitory desires often create confusion about what one "really" desires. Paternalistic prevention measures may be justified by the potential suicide's ignorance about his own deepest desires. However, it would be incorrect to say that the ambivalence alone, or the transitoriness alone, justifies preventive measures; rather, factual ignorance which would otherwise be likely to cause self-harm justifies paternalistic preventive measures. Ambivalence and transitoriness are relevant only as possible sources of ignorance.

One might claim that transitoriness is itself directly relevant to the issue of whether preventive measures would be justified in cases of potential suicide. After all, one may *really* want *now* to kill oneself. However, if this desire would only last for, say, a minute, it may seem that that in itself is relevant to the issue of suicide prevention.

It seems to me that if the transitory desire for suicide accompanied (perhaps by causing) the mistaken belief that the desire is enduring, that would indeed be relevant, but only because that would be an instance of factual error. (Presumably, most people would not act on their suicidal impulses if they were aware of the transitoriness of these impulses.) However, one might press the point by proposing a highly unusual case in which a potential suicide *really* wants to kill himself yet is fully aware that this desire is fleeting. If our potential suicide realizes that his suicidal desire is fleeting and if he is in control of himself, then, unless other-regarding factors are at stake, it seems to me that we are not entitled to prevent his suicide. (I am assuming here that would-be preventers know that the potential suicide has the knowledge and self-control in question. The reason for this will be explained below.) The potential suicide knows that he genuinely wants to kill himself, he knows that his desire is fleeting, and yet he still wants to fulfill the desire. Why should the mere fact that the desire is transient matter in this case when it does not matter in other cases (e.g., cases in which one has transient desires to do tremendous good for society)?

It might be said that in cases of suicidal desire, the transient desire would be terminal if fulfilled. But if death is precisely what the person wants, and if he knows that this desire is fleeting, I fail to see how the *mere* fact of transitoriness counts. Transitoriness is related to factual ignorance (e.g., it may mask one's deeper desires and it might create the illusion that the transitory desire for suicide is actually an enduring desire), but it is only because of this relation that it is relevant to the suicide prevention issue.

Epistemological Arguments

The Unknowable Future: Some have argued that we cannot predict with certainty what any one is likely to experience during the rest of his natural life. The future transcends the limits of human knowledge. What does not yet exist cannot yet be known. Since the future is unknowable, suicide cannot be a rational choice and should therefore be prevented, even if coercive prevention measures are necessary to achieve this end; after all, a cure for the potential suicide's ailments may appear in the near future.[16]

At least one problem with this argument is that rational action does not require certainty about the future; we are forced to act on probabilities. To demand absolute certainty where it cannot be had is itself irrational. In fact, one could easily turn this argument on its head and argue that since one cannot be certain that the next moment will not bring unspeakable agony and degradation, it is irrational to continue living. In fact, if rational action requires certain knowledge with respect to the future, and if such knowledge is beyond our reach, then no action of any kind is rational. We would be forced to accept the conclusion that all actions are irrational.

When we accept the fact that we are forced to act on probabilities, and that certain knowledge of the future is not necessary for rational action, we see at once that suicide may be based on a rational estimate of probabilities and that the action can in fact be rational. I may have a terminal illness that I know will cause me horrific pain. Although it is logically possible that tomorrow a cure will be introduced, this may be hopelessly unlikely, and I may know that this is unlikely by consulting specialists in the field. No one would say, "You shouldn't have your gangrenous foot amputated since it's possible that a miraculous cure will be introduced tomorrow or at least in the very near future." Likewise, no one should say to a potential suicide, "You shouldn't commit suicide to avoid horrible agony since it's at least possible that a miraculous cure will be available in the very near future."

The Logical Opaqueness of Death: A more sophisticated epistemological argument for suicide prevention measures might be developed using the ideas of Philip Devine. Devine argues that a precondition of rational choice is that "one know what one is choosing," either by "experience or by the testimony of others who have experienced it or something very like it." So, "it is not possible to choose death rationally." Nor is any amount of knowledge about what one hopes to escape by death helpful since "*rational choice between two alternatives requires knowledge of both*."[17] Assuming that death is the annihilation of the person (i.e., there is no afterlife), Devine claims that death is "logically opaque" since it is logically impossible for one to experience death or learn about it from the testimony of others who have experienced it or something like it. Devine denies that sleep could give one information about the nature of death since "sleep, even when dreamless, presupposes the continuation of the self in being and the possibility of awakening." Likewise, near-death experiences will not help since "what one would learn about in that way is not death but apparent dying."[18] Since rational choice between two options requires knowledge of both, and since death is unknowable in principle (since no one can experience his own nonexistence), suicide cannot be a rational choice.

Unfortunately, Devine's argument for the claim that one cannot rationally choose death faces several devastating objections.[19] Consequently, no plausible case for suicide prevention can rely on it. As we have seen, he claims that rational choice between two alternatives requires knowledge of both, but since death is logically opaque, suicide cannot be a rational choice. However, Devine's argument would also establish that it is irrational to choose to continue living since the alternative, death, is unknowable. If rational choice between two options requires knowledge of both, then, since by hypothesis death is unknowable, one option in the choice between life and death is unknown. Thus, we reach the absurd conclusion that choosing to live and choosing to die are both irrational choices.

Further, it is sometimes rational to choose an unknown alternative to a known evil; in cases in which a known evil is bad enough, it may be rational to take a chance on an unknown option. For example, if the conditions in one's country are profoundly bad, it may be rational to emigrate to a country about which one knows little or nothing.

Finally, Devine's claim that death is unknowable is itself suspect; if, as he supposes, death is annihilation, it is hard to see what more must be known about it. If we know that death is annihilation, then death's nature is known. Devine's apparent assumption that the knowable must be a species of that which can be experienced is simply false. Clearly, no one can know what it feels like to be dead if death is indeed annihilation; for if death is annihilation, the individual who dies ceases to exist at the point of death and is therefore not in a position to experience his own nonexistence. It is logically impossible to experience one's own nonexistence. However, this shows that the nature of death is unknowable only if we assume that the nature of an event or state of affairs can be known only if it can be experienced. But if one knows that death is the annihilation--the ceasing-to-be--of the individual who dies, one would know the nature of death even though, for logical reasons, one cannot know what it is like to be a nonexistent entity.

Ethical Arguments

The Value of Human Life: Unlike the arguments for the prevention of suicide which have just been considered, what I am calling the ethical arguments for suicide prevention do not rely on special psychological or epistemological claims. Instead, such arguments appeal to undisputable facts (e.g., suicide involves the loss of life) and ethical principles.

We have already come across one such argument: since "*every* human life is of value," "*every* human life is to be saved."[20] Since each human life has intrinsic worth, we are entitled to take whatever measures are necessary to prevent anyone from taking human life.

Even if every human life is of value, it does not follow that every human life is of "absolute value," that its value overrides all other considerations. In the last chapter, we admitted that life has value. But this alone will not justify suicide prevention since we do not accept preventive measures in every case in which someone is considering whether or not to abandon something valuable. Others are not justified in preventing a person from abandoning certain experiences (e.g., instances of pleasure) simply because of the alleged intrinsic value of those experiences. The mere fact that something is valuable does not entail that one can legitimately be forced to accept it.

Other-Regarding Considerations: So far we have focused only on the would-be suicide. One might, however, try to defend suicide prevention measures on the ground that suicide involves deep suffering for others (e.g., the suicide's family and friends). Naturally, one will have to balance this suffering against the negative features of preventive measures; we are not entitled to prevent people from acting in certain ways on the ground that others would be slightly annoyed otherwise. Further, this justification of suicide prevention will not apply to those would-be suicides who do not have important relations to others.

None of the arguments considered justifies preventive measures in all cases of potential suicide. The psychological arguments from mental illness, transitoriness, and ambivalence turned out to be only indirectly relevant; such features alone never justify preventive measures, but they are relevant to the would-be suicide's factual beliefs and self-control. In that sense, mental illness, ambivalence, and the presence of transitory suicidal impulses are indirectly relevant to the issue of suicide prevention. The epistemological arguments proved unsound partly because of their assumptions about rationality. The argument which relies on the claim that the nature of future cannot be known with certainty is flawed because rational action does not require certainty about the future. Any appeal to Devine's view of the "logical opaqueness" of death involves all the problems associated with that view. Further, the mere fact that life is valuable will not justify suicide prevention since we do not accept preventive measures with respect to other actions that involve the abandonment of intrinsic goods. Finally, the argument which tries to justify suicide prevention measures by appealing to other-regarding considerations will justify some instances of prevention, but not all.

The Conditions of Suicide Prevention

Exposing the limitations of these arguments, however, is quite different from discovering the kinds of conditions under which suicide prevention measures are justified. Before discussing suicide facilitation we will consider the kinds of conditions that justify

suicide prevention measures and address some anti-prevention
arguments.

We have already admitted that other-regarding
considerations may justify suicide prevention measures. They may
even make such measures obligatory. If the harm to others would
otherwise be very great, preventive measures may be obligatory.
Further, if suicide would involve the agent in a serious shirking of
duties to others, preventive measures may be justified or even
obligatory, depending on the severity of the violation of duty. Before
we are entitled to interfere in someone's liberty because of that
person's duties to others, however, it seems that the duties in
question must be quite weighty.

Let us ignore other-regarding considerations for the moment
and ask: are we ever justified in preventing suicide because of
factors pertaining only to the would-be suicide? The affirmative
answer seems correct, and we have already indicated one such
factor: the would-be suicide's awareness of non-moral facts.

When a person is about to engage in self-harming behavior,
others are permitted (or perhaps even obliged) to stop him if the
behavior is being undertaken on the basis of factual ignorance. For
example, it is unthinkable that others should idly watch as a person
drinks a poisonous liquid in the belief that it is nonpoisonous. It is
unthinkable that informed persons should do nothing while another
leaps carelessly from an airplane in the mistaken belief that he is
equipped with a parachute. Since suicide involves not only self-harm
but self-killing, suicide prevention measures may be justified if the
suicide's intention to kill himself arises from factual ignorance. In
the literature on suicide, one comes across cases in which individuals
commit suicide because of erroneous factual beliefs. For example, a
person might kill himself in the mistaken belief that he has a
terminal illness. A person who is aware of the individual's health is
justified in preventing the suicide in order to correct the individual's
factual errors.

It might be thought that if an action would serve someone's
interests, then one should not stop that person from performing that
action even if it would cause him harm and would be performed on
the basis of factual ignorance. (An action can be in a person's best
interest and yet cause that person harm: e.g., a painful but
necessary medical procedure might serve one's interests even though
it involves some harm.) However, such a view does not respect the

agent's wish to make informed decisions. For example, plastic surgery might serve a person's interests, but if the patient believes, perhaps because of deception, that he is actually undergoing another operation, it would ordinarily be wrong not to prevent the plastic surgery. Likewise, if I know that walking on a slippery floor might maximize a person's overall self-interest (by allowing him to sue for thousands of dollars), even though a certain amount of harm is involved, I am not ordinarily justified in allowing the person to walk on the slippery portion of the floor.

Sometimes the factual ignorance which justifies suicide prevention concerns the would-be suicide's deepest desires. Even if the agent is informed about all relevant external factors, suicide prevention may be justified when the agent is ignorant about what he "really wants." Here ambivalence and transitoriness play their part; they serve as warning signs to bystanders that the agent may be ignorant about his deepest desires or about the duration of his suicidal desires. However, what counts is the agent's ignorance concerning his own desires, not the agent's ambivalence or the transitoriness of his desires; ambivalence is a symptom of the ignorance in question, while transitory desires may distract one from one's deeper desires.

However, even when a person is suffering from factual ignorance, suicide prevention might still be unjustified. It has been argued that in cases involving an irretrievably psychotic person, the repeated application of suicide prevention measures may be illegitimate even though the patient is suffering from delusions.[21] Suicide prevention measures for psychotic patients may involve extremely degrading procedures. For example, the patient may be completely deprived of privacy of any kind, even the minimal privacy achieved by the wearing of clothing. Even more degrading procedures may be necessary to prevent suicide in such cases. But it seems doubtful that we have the right to degrade the patient to this level. In the case of the irretrievably psychotic patient who has repeatedly expressed his determination to kill himself, the measures necessary to prevent him from doing so involve an unacceptable degree of degradation. I suggest that it would be better to allow the patient to commit suicide, even on the basis of delusions, than to subject him to long-term degradation or pain in the effort to prevent his suicide. So even when the would-be suicide suffers from factual ignorance, preventive measures may not be justified. They will not be so when they involve severe degradation or pain for the potential suicide. This example also brings out the point that to say that suicide prevention is justified in a certain case does not entail that any measure one chooses is justified or that indefinite suicide prevention measures are justified.

The account suggested by our remarks so far is that suicide prevention measures are justified only if (i) the individual's suicidal intentions rest on factual ignorance, or (ii) the agent is not in control of his own behavior, or (iii) suicide would involve the agent in a serious shirking of duties to others and his reasons for suicide do not justify such a violation of duty.

I think, however, that we should add a fourth member to this list: (iv) the individual's suicidal intentions rest on grossly irrational *ethical* beliefs which he would abandon if a bystander were given the chance to enlighten him. Suppose, for instance, that Jones believes that all those who have ever lied are obliged to kill themselves, and he is préparing to act accordingly. It seems that temporary preventive measures are in order. However, if the ethical belief in question is a deeply held conviction which forms part of the core of the potential suicide's ethical viewpoint, interference cannot be justified by the claim that the ethical beliefs are false; ignoring other-regarding considerations, it seems illegitimate to force others to act contrary to their core ethical convictions.[22]

If any of these four conditions is present, *and* the measures do not involve long-term severe pain or degradation, suicide prevention will be justified (assuming the bystander does not have unrelated duties that override his right to prevent the suicide: e.g., the duty to prevent the accidental launching of nuclear weapons). Suicide prevention will be obligatory when it is permissible *and* the bystander is not under an at least equally weighty duty which would require him to allow the suicide. In virtually every case in which preventive measures are permissible, they will also be obligatory.

However, we will have to add a very important qualification to this account. So far, we have assumed that bystanders are aware of the potential suicide's mental state (i.e., his beliefs and level of self-control) and his duties to others. In many cases, however, bystanders will simply have no idea what the would-be suicide's beliefs are, or whether he has strong duties to others, or whether he is in control of himself. For example, if I happen to see a stranger who is about to leap to his death from a bridge, I will ordinarily have no time to come to know his mental state and his duties to others. It seems to me that in cases in which we have no good evidence about the would-be suicide's beliefs or about his duties to others or about his self-control, we should try to prevent the suicide (assuming we do not have unrelated overriding duties that are incompatible with doing so). The reason is that temporarily preventing an informed person who is in control of himself from committing suicide is morally better than doing nothing while, say, a confused person leaps to his death from a bridge, especially since, in all likelihood, the would-be suicide could make another attempt at suicide if this one were prevented and since the suicidal option is irreversible if successful. When we do not know whether or not suicide prevention is justified in the sense discussed in the last paragraph (i.e., when we are ignorant concerning the would-be suicide's beliefs, self-control, or his duties to others), we should try to prevent the suicide since the moral badness of unjustifiably meddling seems less severe than the moral badness of passively allowing a confused or compulsive person to die unnecessarily.

Two Objections

Before summarizing our account of the kinds of circumstances that justify suicide prevention measures, I will consider two objections to suicide prevention. First, Szasz has claimed that suicide prevention involves "a far-reaching infantilization and dehumanization of the suicidal person."[23] We have in effect admitted that in some cases this is so. However, not all suicide prevention measures involve infantilization and dehumanization. If someone is about to kill himself on the basis of the false belief that he has a terminal illness, and I stop him in order to correct his beliefs, this does not involve dehumanization or infantilization. In fact, one might say that I am respecting his deepest wishes, since, presumably, he would not want to die because of easily correctable errors.[24] Szasz has in mind psychiatrists who take any suicidal thoughts as sufficient grounds for extremely coercive and degrading measures. Clearly, he is right to object to this policy. But it would be a mistake to generalize from these instances to the conclusion that all suicide prevention involves degradation and infantilization.

A second objection to suicide prevention, formulated by Robert Martin, asserts that preventive measures with respect to any kind of action are justified only when they spare the agent future regret. But *suicide* prevention does not spare the agent any future regret because, if the suicide were successful, the agent would simply cease to exist; successful suicide attempts cannot result in future regrets. Therefore, suicide prevention is illegitimate. No matter how foolish the decision to commit suicide, preventive measures are not justified since the agent would not thereby be spared future regret. A man who kills himself unaware that treatment was available which could have cured him "won't be worse off than had we intervened, because after his death he won't be *any* way; and because before death he desired death and got it."[25]

This line of reasoning would also force one to accept the conclusion that preventing someone from unknowingly taking a drug that would induce a permanent coma would be illegitimate since one would not spare the person future regret. Further, if a mentally disturbed person decided to attempt flight from the tenth floor, it would be illegitimate to prevent him from doing so; he wanted to fly and will not feel any regrets (being deeply insane, he will not realize the implications of his decision in mid-flight). Clearly, these consequences are unacceptable, but no more unacceptable than Martin's conclusions.

Martin assumes that the potential suicide's present desire is simply for death: "[the suicide] desired death and got it." This, however, is an oversimplification; the suicide's desire is to commit suicide on the basis of knowledge. So by allowing someone to commit suicide on the basis of erroneous factual beliefs, one fails to respect the person's desire for *informed* suicide.[26] (However, as mentioned earlier, it may sometimes be legitimate to let hopelessly psychotic individuals commit suicide even on the basis of their delusions.)

Summary of the Account of Suicide Prevention

We can summarize the account of suicide prevention developed above as follows:

(A)   Where the potential suicide's state of mind (i.e., his beliefs and level of self-control) and his duties to others are known, suicide prevention measures are permissible if and only if the following conditions obtain:

    (1)   At least one of the following is the case: (i) the suicidal intention rests on factual ignorance, (ii) the potential suicide is not in control of his actions, (iii) suicide would involve the suicide in a serious shirking of duties to others which his reasons for suicide do not justify, or (iv) the suicidal intention rests on grossly irrational ethical beliefs which the potential suicide would likely abandon if he were enlightened by a bystander.

    (2)   The preventive measures do not involve long-term and profound degradation or pain for the potential suicide.

(B)   Where the potential suicide's state of mind and his duties to others are known, suicide prevention will be obligatory if and only if

    (1)   it is permissible (since it satisfies the conditions for the permissibility of suicide prevention just rehearsed), and

    (2)   the bystander contemplating preventive measures is not under an at least equally weighty duty which would require him to refrain from preventing the suicide (e.g., the duty to prevent the accidental launching of nuclear missiles).

(C)   Where the potential suicide's state of mind or his duties to others are unknown, temporary preventive measures are called for since, for example, it is better to temporarily prevent an informed person who is in control of his own behavior from committing suicide than to do nothing while a confused or compulsive person kills himself.[27]

Facilitating Suicide

When an informed person who is in control of himself decides to commit suicide, and doing so would be morally permissible, this may create an obligation to assist the suicide. Assuming that the would-be assistant does not have any comparable duties which require him to refrain from assisting the suicide, the considerations which have to be considered are (i) the would-be suicide's ability to commit the act without assistance, (ii) the reasons for suicide, and (iii) the sacrifice assistance would involve for the would-be assistant.

If a person who is morally permitted to commit suicide makes an informed decision to do so, one is not obliged to help that person if he could easily perform the act himself, at least not if doing so would involve personal sacrifice. For instance, if a person is informed that he has a terminal illness and decides to avoid the agony involved by suicide, this may not give rise to a duty to assist since the person might be entirely capable of carrying out the task and since assisting the suicide might seriously undermine one's well-being (e.g., it might result in a prison sentence).

On the other hand, if a person's reasons for suicide are quite weighty, and she cannot do so without assistance, this may make assistance obligatory despite the serious sacrifice it would involve. Whether it will do so depends on the strength of the reasons for suicide and on the depth of sacrifice involved for the would-be assistant. For example, if suicide is a person's only possible escape from horrible and enduring suffering and degradation, and if he cannot bring about his own death without assistance, assistance may be obligatory, even though it would involve serious sacrifice. If the sacrifice consists of a night in jail, assistance would appear to be obligatory. On the other hand, if the sacrifice consists of public execution, assistance seems non-obligatory.

The present legal climate in the United States, in which doctors who assist suicides (e.g., Dr. Jack Kevorkian) face the possibility of criminal prosecution, provides an example of how personal sacrifice may render assistance non-obligatory. In principle, a would-be suicide in need of assistance may have reasons strong enough to create an obligation to assist even though assistance would mean a serious criminal charge and a long prison sentence, though it is admittedly hard to think of a concrete example. Perhaps the case of the general who will reveal precious military secrets unless he kills himself provides an example; one may be obliged to help him commit suicide if he cannot do so otherwise, even though, for some bizarre reason, one would face a prison sentence for doing so.

If the would-be assistant morally disapproves of suicide or of facilitating suicide, should that be seen as relevant to determining whether or not facilitation is obligatory? I think we will have to admit that such disapproval is relevant. Acting in ways which one finds morally unacceptable frequently involves feelings of self-contempt. These negative feelings about oneself have to be considered along with other psychological states that negatively affect one's well-being. The suicide, it seems, cannot legitimately demand that others violate their own ethical principles to help him commit an action which is compatible with his own moral views.

When, then, is assistance obligatory? We have seen that when we focus on permissible suicides, the answer to this question must take into account the potential suicide's reasons for suicide, her capacity to commit the act without assistance, and the sacrifice that would be involved for the would-be assistant. If we assume that the potential suicide could not otherwise commit the act, then determining whether or not assistance is obligatory will be a matter of weighing the reasons for suicide against whatever sacrifice might be involved for the assistant (assuming, of course, that the would-be assistant does not have unrelated overriding duties that are incompatible with assistance). As the reasons for suicide become stronger, the sacrifice for the would-be assistant must also become stronger if assistance is to be non-obligatory. Naturally, there is no easy way to measure the strengths of the reasons for suicide and the sacrifice involved for the would-be assistant.

One might suggest that assistance is obligatory when the sacrifice the would-be suicide would endure without assistance outweighs the sacrifice the would-be assistant would endure by facilitating the suicide. However, I think this is overly demanding. It would require one to assist in the suicide of a person who would otherwise suffer 100 units of pain on some hypothetical pleasure-pain scale, even though assistance would cause one to suffer 99.9 units of pain. Further, even if we did accept this principle, the problem of measurement would not vanish since we cannot precisely measure suffering, degradation, and whatever other factors might negatively affect one's well-being.

We can, however, say that, in cases where the would-be suicide could not otherwise commit suicide, the probability that assistance is obligatory will increase as the reasons for suicide become stronger and as the sacrifices required of the would-be assistant are mitigated. If an individual who could not otherwise commit suicide decides to do so, and the act is morally permissible, then assistance will be obligatory if the reasons for suicide are strong and the sacrifice required is minimal.

Assisting a would-be suicide is merely permissible (i.e., permissible but not obligatory) when doing so would not involve one in a violation of any overriding duties to others. Suicide facilitation, that is, should be treated like any other kind of assistance; it is morally permissible if and only if there are no overriding duties that are incompatible with assistance. Of course, one kind of case in which assistance is not permissible occurs when preventive measures are obligatory for the reasons given in the last section. However, even when prevention is non-obligatory, assisting the suicide might be wrong because of other duties. For example, I am not permitted to assist a suicide if I am under an obligation to save thousands from starvation, an obligation which, we can stipulate, could not be fulfilled if I were to assist the suicide, but I am also not obliged to prevent the suicide.

Two topics need to be addressed at this point. First, the issue of suicide assistance raises the problem concerning possible abuse of permission to assist. Second, we must consider possible effects on the characters of those who facilitate suicide.

One cannot plausibly argue that it is wrong to facilitate a suicide since it is possible for abuses of this privilege to occur, just as one cannot plausibly argue that gynecological practices are wrong since they invite abuse. The possibility that one might exploit acceptance of the idea of facilitated suicide does not affect the moral permissibility (or obligatoriness) of assistance in particular cases. However, the possibility of abuse is relevant to whether we should adopt a *policy* of allowing certain persons (e.g., medical practitioners) to facilitate suicide at their own discretion.

Given that some people have very good reasons for wanting to commit suicide but are incapable of doing so without help, the policy of outlawing all suicide assistance is unjustifiable. That policy mirrors the policy of outlawing all gynecological practices performed by males on the ground that male gynecologists can engage in abuse. Although abuse of this sort occurs, it would be outlandish to solve the problem by forbidding men from practicing gynecology.

Who, then, should assist the suicide? And how can abuses be prevented? The answer to the first question seems to be: experts on death and its causes. In other words, suicide facilitation should be the work of medical practitioners. The answer to the second question is suggested by our attempts to prevent other kinds of abuse. To prevent people from abusing their positions, we often require that their work be supervised. If suicide facilitation could be supervised, that would reduce the risk of abuse. However, as the gynecology example illustrates, supervision does not guarantee the absence of abuse. After all, one cannot rule out the possibility that several people might conspire to engage in abuse.

However, we are going to have to trust someone eventually, unless we are prepared to outlaw all medical practices without exception on the ground that evil doctors might conspire to commit murder for their own amusement while creating the illusion of a "natural death." To demand an absolute guarantee that abuses will not occur is to demand too much. Such a guarantee cannot be given in any field of medicine. Nor can such a guarantee be given outside medicine, as in the military. Why, then, should such a demand be justified in the case of suicide facilitation?

It seems to me that the best policy would be to allow qualified medical practitioners to facilitate suicide when the suicide has made his determination to die known and when the act of facilitation is supervised. To outlaw all suicide facilitation is to adopt a policy which cruelly denies relief to those with very good reasons for suicide who cannot bring about their own deaths without assistance. On the other hand, to adopt an anyone-can-do-it policy toward suicide facilitation invites abuse on a grand scale. Requiring supervision and disclosure seems the best route. (When the individual is incapable of expressing himself because, for example, he is in a coma, we are no longer dealing with the possibility of suicide but with the possibility of involuntary euthanasia, an equally difficult topic.)

Next, we have to consider possible effects on the characters of suicide assistants. One might claim that persons who engage in suicide facilitation are likely to acquire murderous impulses, or that their attitude concerning the value of life will inevitably become warped, or that they may become inclined to suggest suicide as a solution to far too many problems. As evidence of these claims, one might appeal to the fact that Nazi atrocities began with "euthanasia" programs but ended in incredible acts of mass extermination and unfathomable depths of cruelty. However, the comparison is dubious since the so-called "euthanasia" program carried out by the Nazis involved the mass murder of the mentally retarded, the insane, and others who were deemed worthless by Nazi authorities. It was not a voluntary euthanasia policy.

Still, there is a danger that suicide assistants may acquire dangerous tendencies. The solution, once again, is to require some kind of supervision and evaluation. No one would suggest outlawing other branches of medicine on the ground that doctors might acquire a fascination with blood which would lead them to commit murder. No one would suggest that males be prevented from becoming gynecologists on the ground that they might acquire the dangerous tendency to perform involuntary gynecological examinations, or that dental treatment for children should be outlawed since dentists might acquire a taste for inflicting pain on defenseless children.

The danger that suicide assistants might acquire dangerous habits is serious, but this should not lead us to outlaw all suicide facilitation, just as the dangers concerning the habits of other medical practitioners do not lead us to analogous policies with respect to those disciplines. The answer, once again, is to adopt some kind of supervision system. Perhaps frequent psychiatric examinations should be required if the danger that suicide facilitators might acquire unwanted inclinations is in fact quite high.

Conclusion

Suicide prevention measures are justified by the would-be suicide's factual ignorance, by her lack of self-control, by her duties to others, or by the fact that her suicidal intentions rest on grossly irrational ethical beliefs which could be corrected by a bystander. If the intention to kill herself rests on factual ignorance or grossly irrational ethical beliefs, or if the individual is not in control of herself, temporary preventive measures may be justified. If the suicidal individual also has duties to others that would be violated by suicide, preventive measures may also be justified. However, the duties in question must be extremely weighty since we do not think it permissible to interfere in a person's actions simply because he is violating a duty to others. For example, we do not think it legitimate to coercively prevent someone from going to the movies simply because he would thereby violate a minor promise. The conditions under which preventive measures are justified will also make preventive measures obligatory when the bystander does not have an at least equally weighty duty which is incompatible with intervention.

However, we also found that there are limits to the preventive measures which are justified. If preventing an irretrievably psychotic person from committing suicide would require that we permanently subject him to extremely degrading living conditions, such preventive measures are illegitimate, even though the patient's suicidal thoughts rest on psychotic delusions.

We also found that when we do not know whether or not a potential suicide is confused, or whether or not he is in control of his behavior, or whether or not his suicide would constitute a violation of duty, temporary preventive measures should be undertaken, even though one risks intrusion into another's liberty. The reason why preventive measures are recommended in such cases is that the undesirability of temporarily preventing an informed person who is in control of himself from performing a morally permissible action seems less extreme than the undesirability of doing nothing while a confused person, or a person who suffers from compulsions, or a person whose suicide would involve a gross shirking of duty, kills himself, especially since temporary preventive measures would ordinarily allow the would-be suicide to make another attempt and since suicide is a final decision.

With respect to suicide assistance, we found that whether or not assistance is obligatory depends on the would-be suicide's capacity to commit the act without assistance, the reasons for suicide, and the sacrifice assistance would involve for the would-be assistant. Suicide assistance is permissible so long as the would-be assistant does not have overriding duties incompatible with assistance (e.g., a duty to *prevent* the suicide).

To determine whether or not we should prevent or assist a suicide, we should rely on analogies to other actions. For example, we should compare our convictions with respect to preventing someone from accidentally drinking a poisonous liquid with our views concerning the prevention of a suicide that is based on factual ignorance. The goal, once again, should be to make our judgments about suicide in particular cases square with our most deeply held convictions about analogous acts in analogous circumstances.

With respect to the adoption of a suicide facilitation policy, we found that such a policy would be a good thing since it would allow those with good reasons for wanting to die, but who are incapable of bring about their own deaths without assistance, to end their lives. However, the implementation of a suicide facilitation policy must be carefully supervised given the danger that abuses will occur and the danger that suicide assistants will acquire undesirable inclinations or character traits. The potential suicide should also be required to make his determination to die known.

Notes

1. Erwin Ringel, "Suicide Prevention and the Value of Human Life," in *Suicide: The Philosophical Issues*, ed. M.P. Battin and D.J. Mayo (London: Peter Owen, 1980), 206.

2. George Murphy, "Suicide and the Right to Die," *American Journal of Psychiatry* 130 (April 1973): 472.

3. Benjamin B. Wolman ed. *International Encyclopedia of Psychiatry, Psychology, Psychoanalysis, and Neurology* (New York: Aesculapius Publishers, Inc., 1977), s.v. "Suicidal Patients: Hospital Treatment," by Alan A. Stone, 14-15.

4. John Moskop and H. Tristram Engelhardt, "The Ethics of Suicide: A Secular View," in *Suicide: Theory and Clinical Aspects*, ed. L.D. Hankoff and Bernice Einsidler (Littleton: PSG Publishing Co., Inc., 1979), 56.

5. Thomas S. Szasz, "The Ethics of Suicide," in *Suicide: The Philosophical Issues*, ed. M.P. Battin and D.J. Mayo, 186.

6. Jerome A. Motto, "The Right to Suicide: A Psychiatrist's View," in *Suicide: The Philosophical Issues*, ed. M.P. Battin and D.J. Mayo, 212-19.

7. Margaret P. Battin, *Ethical Issues in Suicide* (Englewood Cliffs: Prentice-Hall, 1982), 5.

8. Ibid., 4.

9. Jacques Choron, *Suicide* (New York: Charles Scribner's Sons, 1972), 37.

10. A plausible explanation for our unwillingness to interfere in this kind of case is that paternalistic interference in such cases compromises the person's individuality in that it prevents her from acting on her basic intrinsic values, some of which are of a religious nature. See Elliot D. Cohen, "Paternalism That Does Not Restrict Individuality: Criteria and Applications," *Social Theory and Practice* 12 (1986): 309-335.

11. Edwin S. Shneidman, "Preventing Suicide," in *Suicide: Right or Wrong?*, ed. John Donnelly (Buffalo: Prometheus Books, 1990), 154.

12. Choron, *Suicide*, 50; Battin, *Ethical Issues in Suicide*, 156.

13. Robert M. Martin, "Suicide and False Desires," in *Suicide: The Philosophical Issues*, ed. M.P. Battin and D.J. Mayo, 146.

14. Murphy, "Suicide," 472-73.

15. The example comes from Alan H. Goldman, *Moral Knowledge* (London and New York: Routledge, 1988), 145.

16. Ringel, "Suicide Prevention," 206.

17. Philip E. Devine, "On Choosing Death," in *Suicide: The Philosophical Issues*, ed. M.P. Battin and D.J. Mayo, 139, emphasis added.

18. Ibid., 140-41.

19. David J. Mayo, "The Concept of Rational Suicide," *The Journal of Medicine and Philosophy* 11 (1986): 151.

20. Ringel, "Suicide Prevention," 208.

21. Eliot Slater, "Choosing the Time to Die," in *Suicide: The Philosophical Issues*, ed. M.P. Battin and D.J. Mayo, 202.

22. The claim that the paternalistic restriction of a person's self-regarding conduct is justified only when it does not compromise the individuality of the person by preventing her from acting on her basic intrinsic values is defended in Cohen, "Paternalism."

23. Thomas Szasz, "The Ethics of Suicide," 194.

24. The idea that paternalistic interference may be a way of respecting a person's true wishes is suggested in Ruth Macklin, "Refusal of Psychiatric Treatment: Autonomy, Competence, and Paternalism," in *Psychiatry and Ethics*, ed. R.B. Edwards (Buffalo: Prometheus Books, 1982), 339-40.

25. Robert M. Martin, "Suicide and False Desires," in *Suicide: The Philosophical Issues*, ed. M.P. Battin and D.J. Mayo, 149. Martin admits that other-regarding factors might justify suicide prevention.

26. Arthur M. Wheeler, "Suicide Intervention and False Desires," *The Journal of Value Inquiry* 20 (1986): 241-44.

27. I thank Professors Alan Goldman, Howard Pospesel, and Elliot Cohen for some extremely valuable critical remarks on this section.

CHAPTER 5

SCHOPENHAUER AND CAMUS: SUICIDE AND THE HERO

The history of philosophy contains two thinkers who present particularly unusual conceptions of suicide: Arthur Schopenhauer and Albert Camus. Schopenhauer's views on suicide can be found in his masterpiece of idealistic philosophy, *The World as Will and Representation*,[1] and in the essay "On Suicide," which appears in his collection of miscellaneous writings, *Parerga and Paralipomena*.[2] The principal text for Camus's position is the title essay of *The Myth of Sisyphus*.[3] What unites these authors is their belief that suicide is incompatible with the kind of life led by someone who possesses the kind of character which each author regards as ideal. Both would say a heroic character is incompatible with suicide. However, their conceptions differ regarding the hero's distinctive nature.

I consider the views of Schopenhauer and Camus because their positions are well known and unusual. However, since their views are quite complex, and since they do not claim that suicide is a morally impermissible act--which has been our main concern--but merely that it is somehow an act which the ideal person would not commit, it seems desirable to consider their views after our discussion of the permissibility, impermissibility, or obligatoriness of suicide, suicide prevention, and suicide facilitation. Discussing them previously would have constituted an undesirable digression.

Schopenhauerian Asceticism

There are many beliefs surrounding Schopenhauer's position on suicide that we cannot discuss in detail. I have in mind his extremely bizarre idealistic ontology which considers the world as

111

"will and representation." According to this view, the objects of
sense-experience are "representations," which are conceived as
mental images. But underlying these representations there is the
will-to-live, which is conceived as a single will which "objectifies"
itself in the representations of perceiving subjects. As in the Kantian
system, in Schopenhauer's scheme space, time, and causality apply
only within the phenomenal world, the world we experience in sense-
perception, the world as representation. The will is the "thing-in-
itself," reality as it is independently of our experiences. Thus,
Schopenhauer denies Kant's claim that the thing-in-itself, or reality
as it is independently of our awareness, is wholly unknowable; the
will is reality as it is independently of our awareness.

　　Having said this much, I will not explore the further details
of Schopenhauer's ontology, for this view is simply not a "live
hypothesis" (in the language of William James) for at least virtually
all contemporary philosophers; so far as I know, no contemporary
philosopher accepts the main theses of Schopenhauer's system.
Further, any elaborate discussion of metaphysical abstractions seems
grossly out of place in work of applied ethics. Finally, what is
ethically of interest in Schopenhauer's view of suicide can be isolated
from his general metaphysical view.

　　The first difficulty in understanding Schopenhauer's view of
suicide is that he makes it unclear whether or not he is offering a
moral condemnation of suicide. For example, in "On Suicide" he
dismisses as "wholly meaningless" the claim that suicide is "wrong"
on the ground that "there is obviously nothing in the world over
which every man has such an indisputable *right* as his own person
and life."[4] Further, in *The World as Will and Representation* we are
told that suicide is a "futile and foolish act,"[5] but to call an act futile
and foolish is hardly to offer a moral condemnation. Such passages
may suggest that he offers not a moral condemnation of suicide at
all, but merely a prudential condemnation; suicide fails to achieve
the end at which the suicide aims, although the act is well within
the individual's rights. Although this interpretation is inviting, some
of Schopenhauer's remarks show that he conceives himself as
offering a moral objection to suicide. Schopenhauer claims that he
has provided "the only valid moral reason against suicide."[6] Further,
he points out that his case against suicide "applies only to an ethical
standpoint much higher than that which European moral
philosophers have ever occupied." However, "if we descend from that

very high point, there is no longer any valid moral reason for condemning suicide."[7] In *On the Basis of Morality*, he claims that if "there really are genuine moral motives against suicide, then at all events they lie very deep and are not to be reached by the plummet of ordinary ethics," and he makes clear that he views his own position as providing the "genuine" moral objection to suicide.[8]

I suggest that the solution to these apparent contradictions runs as follows: Schopenhauer holds that (i) suicide is a foolish act because it cannot achieve its aim (this will be explained below), that (ii) suicide is indeed a morally permissible act which is well within one's moral rights,[9] but (iii) the morally ideal type of person will not commit suicide; a morally great human being will refrain from suicide. Schopenhauer claims that the morally ideal person transcends ordinary virtue.[10]

The claim that suicide is permissible may seem inconsistent with the claim that a morally great human being will refrain from suicide. But in fact there is no inconsistency here, just as there is no inconsistency in asserting both that allowing one's talents to rust is morally permissible and that allowing one's talents to rust is not something the morally ideal person would do. A morally ideal person is not merely someone who never commits a wrongful action. A morally ideal person is not merely someone who plays by all the moral rules. Rather, a morally ideal person embodies our image of supreme human excellence. Such a person not only plays by all the moral rules but has an ideal type of character, which is something more. Schopenhauer, I suggest, is concerned not so much with suicide as an act which is either permissible or impermissible (though he clearly espouses its permissibility); he is concerned most of all with claiming that suicide is not an act that a morally ideal person would commit. He is concerned not so much with the permissible/impermissible dichotomy but with the ideal/unideal dichotomy.

Before we consider why the morally ideal person will not commit suicide, we should address Schopenhauer's odd comment that suicide is futile and foolish. He argues that

> since life is always certain to the will-to-live, and
> suffering is essential to life, suicide, or the arbitrary
> destruction of the individual phenomenon, is a quite
> futile and foolish act, for *the thing-in-itself remains*

> *unaffected by it,* just as the rainbow remains
> unmoved, however rapidly the drops may change
> which sustain it for the moment.[11]

The suicide destroys the will's phenomenon, the body, but fails to eliminate the will. In other words, the will is a timelessly eternal striving, but instead of destroying this, the suicide destroys a mere manifestation of the will. Suicide is futile and foolish because the will as timeless thing-in-itself remains "unaffected" by it. Patrick Gardiner explains that in Schopenhauer's view the suicide clearly ends "his existence as an empirical individual, as a particular phenomenon of will, and so destroys his individual consciousness," but "it by no means follows therefrom that he destroys his metaphysical essence," since this (i.e., the will) lies outside time and hence "cannot be extinguished by any act undertaken against the merely phenomenal and therefore temporal objectification of its nature."[12] The suicide wants to escape the torment which the will in him causes him to suffer, and he tries to achieve this end by self-destruction, but instead of destroying the will, he merely eliminates one of its fleeting manifestations. Thus, the suicide can never achieve his goal, since the will is a timelessly eternal thing-in-itself which he action leaves "unaffected."

Rarely has a philosopher launched so metaphysical a critique of the rationality of any action. Schopenhauer's critique of the rationality of suicide can only appeal to those who accept his bizarre ontology, which conceives reality as it is in itself (the thing-in-itself) as a cosmic will. Worse, even if one accepted his general metaphysical system, one could easily void his conclusion that suicide is futile and foolish. For that conclusion relies on the assumption that the suicide is trying to destroy the will as thing-in-itself. So far as I am aware, no suicide note has ever expressed such a metaphysical intention. The goals which most suicides hope to achieve by their deaths can be realized and have nothing to do with a cosmic will. In the words of Michael Fox, a Schopenhauer critic, the successful suicide

> accomplishes exactly what he intended, namely, to
> destroy his individual life, terminate his personal
> consciousness and his suffering, and possibly also to
> cause anguish and/or a guilt reaction in others. So

far from being pointless, his act realizes its purpose
very effectively.[13]

Since Schopenhauer explicitly denies that suicide is wrong,
the only objection to suicide which remains is his claim that the
morally ideal person will refrain from suicide. Schopenhauer tells us
that "suicide is opposed to the attainment of the highest moral goal
since it substitutes for the real salvation from this world of woe and
misery one that is merely apparent."[14] Schopenhauer acknowledges
two ways to escape slavery to the metaphysical will: aesthetic
contemplation and asceticism. In aesthetic contemplation one can
become a disinterested spectator, and this constitutes a temporary
escape from slavery to the will. Schopenhauer claims that the
artistic genius can exhibit "Platonic Ideas" in works of art, and the
aesthetic spectator is thus allowed to contemplate these eternal
Ideas. This disinterested appreciation gives the spectator a period of
rest from slavery to the will. But this relief is fleeting. Therefore, it
does not does constitute a lasting "salvation" from the will.

What constitutes salvation for the individual? For
Schopenhauer, the answer is ascetic denial of the will. Salvation
from the torments of the will can be found only in subjecting the will
to denial: i.e., refusing to gratify it and even acting contrary to its
demands. The individual's only hope of triumphing over the will
consists in countering its demands by refusing to gratify them and
by pursuing goals which the will rejects: "denial has its essential
nature in the fact that the pleasures of life, not its sorrows, are
shunned," and suffering "offers the possibility of a denial of the
will."[15] Schopenhauer is thus led to extol voluntary chastity,
intentional poverty, fasting, and even "self-torture."[16] The
Schopenhauerian ascetic welcomes every suffering that comes to him
as further opportunities to mortify the will which he sees as the
source of the suffering of the world.

The moral objection to suicide is that the suicide, instead of
denying the will, actually affirms it. "Far from being denial of the
will, suicide is a phenomenon of the will's strong affirmation."[17] The
suicide would have liked to gratify the will, but his circumstances
made this impossible. So, he killed himself, not because he had
overcome the will's demands, but because he could not gratify them.
Suicide involves giving in to the will rather than denying it. Instead
of subjecting the will as it appears in him to denial, he merely

eliminates the will's fleeting manifestation: himself. In short, the ideal moral character seeks to conquer the will by opposing its demands (i.e., refusing to gratify it and even acting contrary to its demands). The suicide, on the other hand, wants to gratify the will, for he "wills life, wills the unchecked existence and affirmation [i.e., gratification] of the body; but the combination of circumstances does not allow of these."[18] The suicide would have continued living if his circumstances allowed him to gratify the will. He kills himself instead of facing the task of denying the will.

One might now feel inclined to dismiss Schopenhauer's view of suicide as a hopelessly bizarre by-product of his equally bizarre theory of the "the world as will." However, one can evaluate Schopenhauer's remarks on suicide in abstraction from his general metaphysical position by replacing the metaphysical will with the individual's impulses; instead of viewing the morally ideal person as somehow rising above the metaphysical will, one can view that person as rising above his own impulses. If we consider Schopenhauer's view thus modified, we have to address two questions:

(1)   Is his image of the morally ideal person, even thus modified, an accurate representation of the morally ideal person?

(2)   Is suicide in fact always opposed to Schopenhauer's image of the morally ideal person?

We will consider these questions in turn.

(1) Although Schopenhauer is by no means the only thinker to extol asceticism, the claim that the morally ideal person engages in the asceticism he describes is not a claim which is likely to meet with general acceptance. For example, in Hume's well-known dismissal of the "monkish virtues," of which Schopenhauerian asceticism is certainly a species, such qualities are condemned as neither useful nor pleasurable to anyone. In fact, they are dismissed as vices. Further, Aristotle's account of human excellence would clearly dismiss the suggestion that human excellence is best manifested in such acts as self-torture. However, the best evidence that Schopenhauer's picture of the ideal person is a distorted one can be found in the fact that, were a rational person presented with an actual case of an individual who exemplified Schopenhauerian

asceticism, her response would likely be, not praise or admiration, but shock and even horror. The image of someone who embraces suffering and forgoes all satisfaction and who intentionally impoverishes himself and even subjects himself to torture is not, for most, the image of the ideal person. In fact, in most eyes, such is the image of a fanatic. If somebody is inclined to accept Schopenhauer's ideal, I doubt that any argument would suffice to change his mind. However, I feel confident that most readers will find his presentation of the ideal moral character disturbing rather than accurate.

Admittedly, there is something admirable about the person who can control his impulses, and I am certainly not claiming that the ideal person is a puppet whose actions are mere expressions of his immediate urges. Self-control and moderation are certainly desirable. However, the Schopenhauerian ascetic does not engage in moderation but in self-denial. Nor is the self-control that we find ideal manifested in an act of self-denial which is undertaken for its own sake.

(2) Is suicide in fact incompatible with Schopenhauer's ideal? In a passage which seems to have gone virtually unnoticed,[19] Schopenhauer seems to admit that there is one form of suicide which is compatible with his image of the morally ideal person: "voluntarily chosen death by starvation at the highest degree of asceticism." He admits that

> the complete denial of the will can reach that degree where even the necessary will to maintain the vegetative life of the body, by the assimilation of nourishment, ceases to exist. This kind of suicide is so far from being the result of the will-to-live, that such a completely resigned ascetic ceases to live merely because he has completely ceased to will.[20]

Thus, on Schopenhauer's own admission, suicide is not completely excluded from the morally ideal life. In fact, since he admits that the kind of suicide just described--ascetic suicide through self-starvation--is the act of a "completely resigned ascetic" who has "completely ceased to will," he seems to be forced to admit that suicide by self-starvation at the highest degree of asceticism is an essential element of the morally ideal life. So, not only is suicide not excluded from the morally ideal life, but Schopenhauer's remarks entail that one form of suicide is an essential part of the morally ideal life: ascetic suicide through self-starvation. Far from being a denial of all suicide, Schopenhauer's position affirms one form of suicide. Of course, Schopenhauer is still entitled to claim that all other types of suicide are incompatible with his moral ideal. If his ideal were a plausible one, such a critique would be of considerable importance. However, as we have seen, Schopenhauer's portrayal of the ideal person is implausible.

Camusian Revolt

Camus claims in *The Myth of Sisyphus* that "suicide is not legitimate."[21] As will become clear in what follows, by this comment he does not seem to mean that suicide is morally impermissible, although, unlike Schopenhauer, Camus does not explicitly say that suicide is morally permissible. (Schopenhauer, it will be recalled, denied that suicide is wrong; such a claim is "meaningless" since each person has rights over his own person.) Instead, the suicide is said to lack the "majesty"[22] of the person who refrains from suicide in the face of the absurdity of human existence; to face the absurdity of human existence, rather than to commit suicide, involves "something exceptional."[23] These remarks suggest not that suicide is impermissible, but that the truly ideal person will not commit suicide, which, as we have seen, is a distinct claim.

Further evidence for my claim that Camus is not asserting that suicide is morally impermissible can be found in his conception of what the "problem of suicide" is. He claims, as is well known, that the problem of suicide is the "only truly serious philosophical problem."[24] But the problem of suicide which he considers so important is not, he makes clear, the problem of determining whether or not suicide is morally permissible. Instead, the problem of suicide is said to be the problem of determining "whether life is or is not worth living."[25] He claims that the subject of *The Myth of Sisyphus* is the relationship "between the absurd and suicide, the exact degree to which suicide is a solution to the absurd."[26]

I will, therefore, proceed on the assumption that Camus, like Schopenhauer, is concerned not so much (or even at all) with the permissible/impermissible dichotomy as it applies to suicide; rather, he is concerned with the ideal/unideal dichotomy as it applies to suicide. However, in order to understand why he views suicide as an unideal act, his views concerning the absurdity of human existence must be understood, since Camus's ideal person is one who adopts a special attitude towards the alleged absurdity of human existence.

Camus repeatedly claims that "the absurd" consists of a conflict between human demands or desires and the world. The absurd is the conflict between "what man wants" and "what the world offers him."[27] So, in order to know what the absurdity of human existence consists in, we must know what Camus believes people want and what he believes "the world" denies them.

We are told that human beings are driven by a "desire for unity."[28] They desire to understand the world "in a single principle." For example, the Greek philosopher Parmenides tried to understand reality as a single entity: "the One."[29] We are also driven by a "wild longing" for intelligibility in the world.[30] Our desire to find intelligibility in the world would be satisfied if we found that the universe is like us--if, for example, "man realized that the universe like him can love and suffer."[31]

But what does the world offer which conflicts with our demands for cosmic unity and intelligibility? First, the universe fails to satisfy our demand for cosmic unity; for if "we assert with Parmenides the reality of the One (whatever it may be), we fall into the ridiculous contradiction of a mind that asserts total unity and proves by its very assertion its own difference and the diversity it meant to resolve."[32] Second, the world frustrates our quest for intelligibility. Camus claims that, although the self's various "aspects" (e.g., its traits, its development) can be enumerated, the self transcends our knowledge: "For if I try to seize this self of which I feel sure, if I try to define and to summarize it, it is nothing but water slipping through my fingers." The quest for the self is doomed to frustration: "Forever I shall be a stranger to myself."[33] Further, the scientific understanding of the universe resorts to "poetry" and "metaphor" since it teaches of "an invisible planetary system in which electrons gravitate around a nucleus." In fact, "I realize that if through science I can seize the phenomena and enumerate them, I cannot, for all that, apprehend the world."[34] "The world itself, whose single meaning I do not understand, is but a vast irrational."[35]

The absurd, then, "depends as much on man as on the world" since it is the "confrontation of this irrational [i.e., the world] and the wild longing for clarity whose call echoes in the human heart."[36] Since the human demands for intelligibility and unity in the universe are frustrated by the universe, human existence is absurd. The absurdity of human existence consists in this tension between human desires and "the unreasonable silence of the world."[37]

Having concluded that human existence is absurd, Camus considers possible ways in which one might respond to the absurdity of human existence. One method, which he calls "philosophical suicide," consists in a "leap" of faith wherein one believes, despite the evidence to the contrary, that the universe is intelligible and unified. However, Camus dismisses philosophical suicide as unauthentic--as involving "deceit" and "subterfuge" rather than "integrity."[38] On the other hand, the "absurd man" (Camus's ideal) commands himself to "live *solely* with what he knows, to accommodate himself to what is, and to bring in nothing that is not certain."[39]

As for suicide proper, Camus dismisses it as a response to the absurd, since living with the knowledge of the absurdity of one's existence constitutes a kind of "metaphysical revolt" in which the rebel lives in defiance of the absurd. Such a person manifests human excellence:

> That revolt gives life its value. Spread out over the whole length of a life, it restores its majesty to that life. To a man devoid of blinders, there is no finer sight than that of the intelligence at grips with a reality that transcends it. The sight of human pride is unequaled. No disparagement is of any use. That discipline that the mind imposes on itself, that will conjured up out of nothing, that face-to-face struggle have something exceptional about them.[40]

The suicide, unlike the absurd man, capitulates when faced with the absurdity of human existence. "The absurd man," on the other hand, "can only drain everything to the bitter end, and deplete himself."[41] Camus appeals to the story of Sisyphus, who was condemned by the gods to the endless task of rolling a boulder to the top of a mountain, only to have it roll down again. We are told that Sisyphus is "the absurd hero" since he is "superior to his fate," and there is "no fate that cannot be surmounted by scorn."[42]

What can we make of this position? I will offer several remarks on Camus's position regarding the absurdity of human existence and his related claims regarding suicide.

(1) Camus's argument for the absurdity of human existence is hardly compelling. We are told that human existence is absurd since human desires for intelligibility and unity are frustrated by the universe's unintelligibility and disunity. This raises at least two problems.

(i) With respect to the desire for cosmic unity, we can admit that scientists sometimes try to reduce the kinds of entities they espouse, and some philosophers have indeed argued that "all is one" in some sense. However, few people would be horrified by the thought that the universe contains more than one irreducible kind of substance or that reality does not consist of a single entity like the Parmenidean One. The average person is simply not a victim of the urge for cosmic unity which Camus describes. If there is a desperate urge for cosmic unity, it must be felt by a select few. Whoever is unconcerned about cosmic unity will not be troubled to learn that the universe does not exhibit such unity. The absurdity of such a person's life will, therefore, have to derive from some other source.

(ii) As for the desire for intelligibility, Camus cannot plausibly claim that the universe is wholly unintelligible. In fact, scientific knowledge, however incomplete, is quite impressive. So, if there is a conflict between our desire for intelligibility and the world, our desire must be for full or total intelligibility. Otherwise the universe might satisfy our desire for intelligibility and no conflict would result. However, it is extremely doubtful that human beings essentially have this need. Admittedly, some people crave intelligibility and are dissatisfied upon being told that some fact must simply be accepted without explanation. Some philosophers have even ventured to assert that there are no brute facts; according to the "principle of sufficient reason," there is an explanation for each and every fact. But if we set aside extravagant metaphysicians and others who crave intelligibility, we see at once that most people are quite happy simply to accept facts as given, however arbitrary they may be. If there is a demand for full intelligibility, it cannot be a demand which most people bother to make. Once again, Camus is simply wrong in claiming to have discovered needs which human beings essentially possess.

In order to justify his claim that the universe frustrates our demand for intelligibility, Camus asserts that knowledge of the self is impossible and that science resorts to poetry and metaphor in its account of the ultimate constituents of matter. Admittedly, self-knowledge is hard to come by since, for example, we are strongly inclined to interpret our motives in the most flattering way. Years of psychoanalysis have proved insufficient for many patients seeking self-discovery. It is also true that the concept of a self is hard to pin down, and if we conceive the self as an immaterial substance, then, as Hume noted, the self is not an object of experience. Further, we can admit that much of science has become unintelligible to scientific laymen. And the process of explanation may stop at arbitrary, brute facts whose existence we simply have to accept without explanation. The world, then, may exhibit unintelligibility to a certain degree. But it is certainly not the case that the universe eludes human comprehension in every respect. And most people never demand more intelligibility from the world than it is willing to grant.

(2) Suppose we grant that human beings crave more intelligibility from the universe than the universe is willing to grant, and let us even suppose (implausibly) that this is an essential desire in human beings, so that there is no chance of living without it. If human existence is absurd in this sense, I see no reason for believing that the absurdity of human existence has any important relation to suicide. For once the absurdity of human existence is interpreted as meaning only that the human need for intelligibility cannot be satisfied, I see no reason to accept the claim that the absurdity of human existence, so construed, calls for any reaction which is incompatible with suicide. Why should the mere conflict between our demand for intelligibility and reality, which Camus insists on calling "the absurd," merit anything so dramatic as "metaphysical revolt," in which one ponders the conflict just mentioned and responds to it with an attitude of scornful defiance? Consider the following analogy. Suppose Jones argues that because human beings desire lives of uninterrupted happiness even though the nature of the world inevitably frustrates such desires, human life must be characterized as absurd and the appropriate response is one of defiance, revolt, and scorn. Such absurdity, it seems clear, does not call for defiance, revolt, or scorn. Likewise, the absurdity which consists in the alleged

unsatisfiability of our desire for intelligibility simply does not call for an attitude of defiance. Camus's insistence that one live in scornful defiance of the absurd to the bitter end seems to require a Wagnerian reaction to a situation which does not merit a dramatic response. This kind of criticism of Camus is suggested in Thomas Nagel's important article "The Absurd"; the alleged absurdity of human life, Nagel tells us, need not "evoke a defiant contempt that allows us to feel brave or proud. Such dramatics, even if carried on in private, betray a failure to appreciate the cosmic unimportance of the situation."[43]

Our critique of Camus's position on suicide thus far can be summarized as follows: (1) Camus's description of the absurdity of human existence is implausible since most people simply lack the needs which, on Camus's view, generate the absurd: the need for cosmic unity and the need for full intelligibility, or at least for a level of intelligibility which the universe is unwilling to grant. Some may want to view the universe in this way, but even they seem capable of eliminating such needs if they realize that their satisfaction is impossible. Camus may be right in asserting that the universe is not fully intelligible since some aspects of the universe may be beyond our comprehension and some facts may be arbitrary. However, once again, most people lack desires for complete, or even relatively complete, intelligibility. Instead, most people never demand more intelligibility from the world than it is willing to grant. In fact, most people demand far less. So, even if the universe is partially unintelligible, this will not bother most people. (2) Even if we grant that human beings essentially crave intelligibility from a world which fails to meet this need, it seems clear that such a state of affairs does not call for metaphysical revolt, an attitude of defiance in the face of the absurd. The absurdity of human existence, so construed, calls for no such dramatic response. The absurdity of human existence does not call for any response which would require one to refrain from suicide.

However, some have argued that Camus's notion of the absurdity of human existence is not grounded primarily in the conflict between the alleged human needs for cosmic unity and intelligibility and the disunity and unintelligibility of the world, despite Camus's emphasis on that conflict. Instead, the absurdity of human existence consists primarily of the conflict between, on the one hand, human religious desires for immortality and the existence of God, and, on the other hand, mortality and God's nonexistence. Camus believes that people yearn for God and immortality, but, unfortunately, God and immortality are fictions. The absurdity of human existence consists mainly of this conflict between human religious needs and the fictitious character of the objects of these needs.[44]

On this view, the objection to suicide would be that the suicide capitulates before the facts of Godlessness and mortality instead of facing these facts with an attitude of scornful defiance. Such defiance is the heroic response to the absurdity of human existence. The suicide is too weak to bear the tragic facts of Godlessness and personal annihilation. The hero lives in defiance of these facts.

This certainly makes Camus's position more plausible, since the nonexistence of God and personal mortality are more serious disappointments for many than the fact that the universe is not wholly intelligible or the fact that it fails to manifest cosmic unity. Further, Camus claims that absurdity is "an invitation to death."[45] But the partial unintelligibility of the universe and its disunity hardly make death appealing for most people. On the other hand, the nonexistence of God and the prospect of personal annihilation can result in profound disappointment which might make death appealing as a quick end to an existence which is condemned to eventual annihilation anyway. Unfortunately, however, there are problems even with this version of the absurdity of human existence and the related critique of suicide.

(1) Although many people yearn for God and eternal life, these are hardly essential desires. Many people find the idea of God rather bizarre and feel no need for such a being. Likewise, most people are too caught up in the task of living earthly lives to concern themselves with immortality. Some people find these religious notions so fantastic that they regard them as unworthy of serious consideration. Some philosophers have even claimed that they would be seriously disappointed to learn that their existence will be everlasting. Thus, Camus is simply mistaken in claiming that these religious desires are essential aspects of human nature.

(2) Not all suicide is undertaken as a response to the absurd, and people often refrain from suicide for reasons having nothing to do with the existence or nonexistence of God or immortality. Camus claims that suicide is an unheroic response to the absurd, but many

suicides are simply not responses to the absurd at all. Many suicides are undertaken for far less metaphysical reasons. For example, for those suicides who believe in, or at least do not deny, survival of bodily death and God, suicide is clearly not undertaken as a response to mortality and God's nonexistence. Camus seems to follow Schopenhauer in interpreting the motives behind all suicide in terms of his own philosophical theory, but such a practice will lead us to misinterpret most suicides. (A similar point applies to the previous interpretation of the absurdity of human existence, for suicide is rarely undertaken as a response to the conflict between our desires for cosmic unity and intelligibility and the disunity and unintelligibility of the universe.)

(3) Camus claims that the proper response to the conflict between religious desires for God and immortality and the facts of Godlessness and mortality is not suicide but some kind of scornful defiance or revolt. Camus describes the revolt he extols as "the certainty of a crushing fate, without the resignation that ought to accompany it," and he adds that the absurd man "is the contrary of the reconciled man."[46] However, does the conflict which he discusses call for any such dramatic response? One wonders why the most appropriate response is not simply the abandonment of these desires. Are these desires which we cannot live without? Obviously this is not the case since so many people manage to live without them. Even supposing that such desires are part of human nature, which is clearly not the case, acceptance of the facts seems to be the desirable reaction. Admittedly, there are situations in which we admire those who exhibit scornful defiance. For example, one might admire the slave or concentration camp inmate who exhibits an attitude of scornful defiance towards his tormentors. But to adopt an attitude of scornful defiance towards anything but a conscious being seems as inappropriate as hurling insults at the rain for ruining one's picnic. When the facts in question are impersonal aspects of the universe--in this case, Godlessness and mortality--an attitude of scornful defiance is pathological, or at least hopelessly misguided. Camus's hero is even said to maintain the absurd "constantly" by contemplating it.[47] One is given the image of a person obsessed with the vanity of human religious wishes. To repeat, this is not the image of a hero but of a maladjusted individual, a person worthy, perhaps, of psychotherapy, but certainly not awe. If God does not exist and death means personal annihilation, and if one essentially

has needs for God and immortality (which is not the case), the most appropriate response is acceptance of these facts. Acceptance of these facts is, however, compatible with committing suicide for reasons which are unrelated to the alleged absurdity of human existence. One might commit suicide for reasons which have nothing to do with despair over God's nonexistence or one's own mortality.

(4) As we have seen, Camus claims that the absurdity of one's life consists in a relation between one's desires and the world. The most heroic response to the absurdity of one's life is, according to Camus, an attitude of scornful defiance in which one refuses to reconcile oneself to the absurd. However, it seems to me that since the absurdity of one's life depends on a conflict between one's desires and the world, the suicide who conceives of his action in Camusian terms can go beyond the Camusian hero in his attitude of scornful defiance towards the absurdity of his own life. For while the Camusian hero simply refuses to resign himself to the absurdity of his life, the suicide actually destroys it. The suicide can conceive of his action as the *self-sacrificial annihilation of the absurdity of his own life*. I submit that, in a Camusian scheme, the most heroic response to the absurd is not the mere refusal to resign oneself to the absurd but the self-sacrificial annihilation of the absurdity of one's own life through suicide. Far from showing that suicide is not an unideal act, Camus's ideas can be used to argue that suicide is an essential part of the most ideal response to the absurd. (However, as we have seen, the alleged absurdity of human life in fact calls for no dramatic response, either in the form of metaphysical revolt or a suicidal assault on the absurd.)

Before concluding, we should note that Nagel offers yet another conception of the absurdity of human existence, a conception which he claims is more plausible than that offered by Camus. Nagel agrees that the absurdity of human existence consists in a conflict, but the conflict is not between our expectations and the world. Instead, the absurdity of human existence consists in "the collision between the seriousness with which we take our lives and the perpetual possibility of regarding everything about which we are serious as arbitrary, or open to doubt."[48] Although we ordinarily take our pursuits very seriously, we can, Nagel claims, view our lives "*sub specie aeternitatis*." From this vantage point, all our pursuits seem arbitrary and unimportant. Nevertheless, we do not abandon our pursuits, "and there lies our absurdity: not in the fact that such an external view can be taken of us, but in the fact that we ourselves can take it, without ceasing to be the persons whose ultimate concerns are so coolly regarded."[49]

This account of the absurdity of human life may be considered more plausible than that proposed by Camus, although one might have doubts about the possibility of viewing one's life from a god's point of view. However, the absurdity of human life, so construed, is, as Nagel himself points out, not a problem to which we need to find a solution. Although our lives may be absurd in this sense, no dramatic response (e.g., suicide or scornful defiance) is called for. Instead of responding to the absurdity of our lives with scornful defiance, Nagel suggests, more plausibly, that "we can approach our absurd lives with irony instead of heroism or despair."[50]

Conclusion

Neither Schopenhauer nor Camus succeeds in showing that suicide is essentially an unideal act, that a moral hero will never resort to suicide. Both present distorted images of human excellence. Schopenhauer presents us with a self-abusive ascetic, while Camus presents us with a mind which defiantly obsesses over the conflict between its intellectual and religious desires and the world. Further, Schopenhauer is forced to admit that the height of asceticism involves a form of suicide: suicide through self-starvation. Similarly, since the absurd, on Camus's view, consists in a relation between desires and the world, one might claim that the self-sacrificial destruction of the absurdity of one's life through suicide is actually more heroic than "metaphysical revolt." Thus, there are resources within both philosophies which can be appropriated by someone seeking to show that the ideal life involves suicide.

Notes

1. Arthur Schopenhauer, *The World as Will and Representation*, vol. 1, trans. E.F.J. Payne (New York: Dover Publications, Inc., 1969).

2. Arthur Schopenhauer, *Parerga and Paralipomena*, vol. 2, trans. E.F.J. Payne (Oxford: Oxford University Press, 1974), 306-311.

3. Albert Camus, *The Myth of Sisyphus and Other Essays*, trans. Justin O'Brien (New York: Vintage Books, 1983).

4. Schopenhauer, "On Suicide," 306.

5. Schopenhauer, *The World*, 399.

6. Schopenhauer, "On Suicide," 309.

7. Ibid.

8. Arthur Schopenhauer, *On the Basis of Morality*, trans. E.F.J. Payne (Indianapolis: Bobbs-Merrill Co., Inc., 1965), 60; also footnote 11.

9. Unfortunately, Schopenhauer seems to defend this claim by arguing that one's life is one's property, an argument that we criticized in Chapter 3.

10. Schopenhauer, *The World*, 380. Schopenhauer means that ordinary virtue does not involve asceticism, which, as we shall see, is characteristic of the morally ideal person.

11. Ibid., 399, emphasis added.

12. Patrick Gardiner, *Schopenhauer* (Baltimore: Penguin Books, 1963), 288.

13. Michael Fox, "Schopenhauer on Death, Suicide and Self-Renunciation," in *Schopenhauer: His Philosophical Achievement*, ed. Michael Fox (Brighton, UK: Harvester Press, 1980), 168.

14. Schopenhauer, "On Suicide," 309.

15. Schopenhauer, *The World*, 398, 399.

16. Ibid., 382.

17. Ibid., 398.

18. Ibid.

19. Frederick Copleston seems to be one of the few exceptions. See Frederick Copleston, *Arthur Schopenhauer: Philosopher of Pessimism* (London: Search Press, 1975), 177.

20. Schopenhauer, *The World*, 401.

21. Camus, *The Myth of Sisyphus*, v.

22. Ibid., 55.

23. Ibid.

24. Ibid., 3.

25. Ibid.

26. Ibid., 6.

27. Ibid., 30.

28. Ibid., 51, also 17.

29. Ibid., 17.

30. Ibid., 21.

31. Ibid.

32. Ibid., 17-18.

33. Ibid., 19.

34. Ibid., 20.

35. Ibid., 27.

36. Ibid., 21.

37. Ibid., 28.

38. Ibid., 50.

39. Ibid., 53.

40. Ibid., 55.

41. Ibid., 55.

42. Ibid., 120-21.

43. Thomas Nagel, "The Absurd," *The Journal of Philosophy* 68 (1971): 727.

44. Joseph McBride, *Albert Camus: Philosopher and Litterateur* (New York: St. Martin's Press, 1992), 3-8.

45. Camus, *The Myth of Sisyphus*, 64.

46. Ibid., 54, 59.

47. Ibid., 54-55.

48. Nagel, "The Absurd," 718.

49. Ibid., 720.

50. Ibid., 727.

EPILOGUE

Perhaps the most important point unearthed by this study is the moral complexity of suicide. Deciding whether or not a particular suicide is morally permissible or even obligatory is hard work. Likewise, persons who are exposed to potential suicides face a number of issues that are often quite difficult to settle. The method to be employed consists in using analogies of various sorts, as we did several times in the course of this work. This method allows us to compare our views on suicide with our views on analogous actions. For example, we can compare the policy of outlawing all suicide facilitation on the ground that it invites abuse to the policy of outlawing certain respected medical professions for the same reason.

We have found that all-or-none approaches (e.g., "All suicide is wrong," "No suicide is wrong," "All suicide should be prevented," etc.) are too simplistic, although they are certainly easy to apply. A more centrist view is required. First, as we saw, although some suicide is wrong (because of overriding duties to others), not all is. In some cases, individual rights justify suicide even in the face of duties to others. Second, while it is obvious that not all suicide is obligatory, some is obligatory since duties to others may require it, just as duties to others often require other kinds of personal sacrifice. Third, suicide prevention measures are sometimes justified (or even obligatory), but the tyrannical position adopted by some psychiatrists, the view that all suicide must be prevented at whatever cost to the potential suicide, is mistaken. Finally, with respect to suicide facilitation, we found that such facilitation is sometimes justified (or even obligatory), while in other cases it is not, since, for example, preventive measures are in order. We also found that a policy whereby certain medical practitioners are allowed to facilitate suicide should take into account possible abuse and possible negative effects on the characters of those who assist suicide.

In one sense it is unfortunate that the all-or-none approaches are mistaken, for these views would save us from the difficult moral tasks which our moderate view demands. Simply by knowing that a particular act would be an instance of suicide, one could know whether or not it is morally permissible, and whether or not others are justified in preventing or assisting the suicide. Perhaps the desire to avoid having to make difficult moral choices is largely responsible for the appeal of such positions in the eyes of many. Unfortunately, truth need not cater to human convenience.

We also considered the unusual positions adopted by Schopenhauer and Camus. Both argue, though on different grounds, that suicide is not the ideal response to the human condition. However, we found that their descriptions of the ideal character are flawed. Schopenhauer presents us with a self-abusive ascetic, while Camus presents us with a character who obsesses defiantly over the absurdity of human existence, even though such absurdity, even if actual, calls for no dramatic response. Further, we found that there are resources within the philosophies of Schopenhauer and Camus which can be used to show that both philosophers should endorse suicide as an essential part of the ideal life. Schopenhauer is forced to admit that ascetic suicide through self-starvation is the ideal mode of death, while Camus seems forced to admit that the self-sacrificial annihilation of the absurdity of one's own life manifests the highest form of scornful defiance concerning the absurd.

APPENDIX

DEFINING SUICIDE

The definition of the term "suicide" is a hotly debated issue. Various authors have proposed different conditions which an act must satisfy before it can be counted as a case of suicide. Proponents of a certain definition will object to other proposals on the ground that they do not harmonize with "common sense intuitions" about what acts do, and what acts do not, count as cases of suicide.

The practice of trying to find a precise set of conditions such that all rational people will agree that an act counts as suicide if and only if it satisfies those conditions rests, it seems to me, on some naive assumptions. First, it rests on the assumption that the concept of suicide is not vague, that it has sharp boundaries which can be discovered--rather than manufactured--through hard philosophical work. But why assume this? After all, most of us learned the use of the word "suicide" from people who never gave a thought to the task of giving a precise meaning to the term. While philosophers sometimes demand precise definitions of terms, most people are satisfied with a certain amount of vagueness. A second naive assumption that philosophers habitually make is that there is *one* concept of suicide to be discovered. Why should we even expect that a concept which each of us internalizes under different circumstances from different people will be identical in each person's conceptual repertoire? Since each of us comes to use the term "suicide" under different circumstances, and since we pick up this word from people who probably never even thought about giving a precise meaning to the term, it seems incredibly naive for philosophers to assume that we can discover *the* concept of suicide. Of course, there is a great deal of overlap between the ways different people use the word "suicide," but it is folly to expect total uniformity in the use of this term.

Having said this, I will now defend a definition of "suicide." I excuse myself by noting that my goal is neither to discover a perfectly precise definition--a task which, as we will see, is probably hopeless--nor to discover a definition which will satisfy everyone, or even every rational person. Experience suggests that the latter attempt is as futile as the former. Rather, I want to clarify a definition which seems to capture, at least roughly, what most people would regard as the essence of suicide.

I will defend what I call an "Intentional Analysis" of suicide. Although there are numerous analyses that fall under this heading, all share the insight that the concept of suicide must be analyzed in terms of the intentions of the agent committing suicide. Before considering the kind of analysis I favor, however, I will briefly consider some influential definitions which seem inadequate for various reasons.

Some Inadequate Accounts

Self-killing: According to the Self-Killing Analysis, a person has committed suicide if and only if he has killed himself.[1] To commit suicide involves nothing more than self-killing.

That this analysis is too wide (i.e., includes cases which should not be classed as suicides) is shown by the fact that it mistakenly includes Case A below as a suicide:

Case A:

> While cleaning a loaded rifle, Al accidentally pulls
> the trigger, thereby killing himself.

Here we have a clear case of accidental self-killing, not a suicide, but the account in question mistakenly classes Al as a suicide. So the Self-Killing Analysis is too wide.

Self-murder: According to the Self-Murder Analysis, "suicide" is synonymous with "self-murder," which is "morally wrong by definition."[2] This is actually an Intentional Analysis of the concept of suicide, for the concept of murder which it contains is defined in terms of the intentions of the agent.

Nevertheless, I think we have good reason to reject such an approach. If part of what it means to call an act suicide is that the act is morally wrong, then clearly the present work and countless others are hopelessly misguided. The question "Is every suicide wrong?" will be as easy to answer affirmatively as the question "Are all bachelors single?" This analysis simply fails to explain why so many intelligent people have asked themselves in all seriousness whether there are any cases of suicide which are not morally wrong. Surely those who have denied that all cases of suicide are morally wrong are not mistaken *by definition.*

Durkheim's definition: Besides Intentional Analyses, the most influential account of suicide was formulated by sociologist Emile Durkheim. According to this view, "suicide" applies to *"all cases of death resulting directly or indirectly from a positive or negative act of the victim himself, which he knows will produce this result."*[3] Like Intentional Analyses and unlike the Self-Killing Analysis, Durkheim's approach involves reference to a mental state or disposition of the agent: knowledge. However, for reasons which will be discussed in our treatment of Intentional Analyses, Durkheim explicitly rejected any analysis which made reference to intentions.

It may be thought that the problem with Durkheim's analysis is that it allows the victim's death to result from a "negative act"; that is, this analysis allows the victim's death to result from a decision to refrain from doing something, and perhaps this renders it defective. Two examples adapted from the literature, however, are sufficient to show that Durkheim was right to allow for the possibility of negative suicide:

Case B:

> Bob needs a routine, safe, and painless operation, which, however, is necessary to save his life. He has no abnormal fear of operations. Nevertheless, he has come to believe that his life is totally meaningless; it is characterized by intense suffering which is unrelated to the condition which necessitates the operation. In order to end it all, Bob refuses the operation and dies.[4]

Case C:

> Chuck has accidentally swallowed a poisonous liquid.
> While being offered a simple antidote, he reflects on
> the likely failure of most of his life's endeavors. He
> decides to take advantage of the poison in his blood
> stream and refuses the antidote. Moments later,
> Chuck is dead.[5]

Bob and Chuck have both caused their own deaths by
committing so-called negative acts. Nevertheless, both have
committed suicide. Thus, we must follow Durkheim and allow for the
possibility of negative suicide.
        However, the Durkheimian Analysis is too wide; one can
knowingly cause one's death, or knowingly place oneself in
circumstances which cause one's death, without thereby committing
suicide. Consider the following case:

Case D:

> A doctor volunteers to render medical aid to a
> plague-infested village. Given the nature of the
> plague, the doctor knows that she will die as a result
> of her visit. She decides that the suffering of the
> villagers must be mitigated at all cost. A few days
> after treating the villagers, our doctor dies of the
> plague.[6]

Case D counts as a case of suicide on Durkheim's definition,
but surely this is a mistake. As Holland has put it, on this account
"it looks as if we have to say that a man who exposes himself to
mortal danger, for whatever reason and whatever the circumstances,
is exposing himself to suicide" so long as the man knows what he is
doing.[7] Durkheim's analysis, then, is too wide since it is satisfied by
acts which do not count as cases of suicide. It is possible to
knowingly place oneself in fatal circumstances without thereby
committing suicide.

Towards an Intentional Analysis

The current dispute concerning the definition of "suicide" is, in general, a dispute between supporters of various Intentional Analyses. There is general, though of course not universal, agreement that the concept of suicide cannot properly be analyzed without reference to the suicide's intentions. In this section, I will defend an Intentional Analysis of suicide. The definition I endorse is a slightly modified version of the definition offered by Michael Wreen, who presents an excellent discussion of this issue.[8]

The simplest Intentional Analysis would run as follows:

Person S commits suicide at time T if and only if

(1)   S intends at T to kill himself, and

(2)   S acts at T in such a way as to kill himself.

That this analysis is too wide is shown by its inclusion of the following case as an instance of suicide:

Case E:

> Elsa intends to shoot herself at about noon. But she decides to clean her gun first to make sure that all goes as planned. Just as she is about to finish--about noon--she sneezes, accidentally pulls the trigger, and kills herself.

Clearly, Elsa has not committed suicide, although she intended to kill herself at about noon and did kill herself at about noon. Thus, the present analysis is too wide.

The problem in Case E is that the intention was not connected in the appropriate way with the events which brought about the agent's death. Perhaps, then, the definition can be corrected simply by adding a further condition:

(3)   The intention specified in (1) causes (through a number of generated actions) the action described in (2).[9]

Condition (3) includes the notion of "generated actions," a concept developed in great detail by Alvin Goldman in *A Theory of Human Action*.[10] It is impossible to give a full account of this here, but we can clarify the concept sufficiently for our purposes.

Sometimes two particular actions ("act-tokens") A and A* are related in such a way that it is appropriate to say that an agent did A* *by* doing A. When this occurs, A is said to "generate" A*. Some of Goldman's examples should make this clearer. According to Goldman, in certain situations, the following generation relations obtain:[11]

(a)   John's moving his hand *generates* John's moving his queen to king-knight-seven.

(b)   John's shooting the gun *generates* John's killing George.

(c)   John's extending his arm *generates* John's signaling for a turn out the car window.

(d)   John's asserting that p *generates* John's contradicting his earlier statement.

Assuming the surrounding conditions are appropriate (e.g., John is in a country where extending one's arm out of a car window is the conventional way of signaling for a turn), it is appropriate to say in each case that John performs the second action *by* performing the first. Where this is the case, the first action is said to generate the second.

Do conditions (1)-(3) constitute an adequate analysis of suicide? Wreen offers a counterexample to the account developed thus far:

Case F:

> [Felix], a man down on his luck, living in a condemned, run-down building, might come to believe that the only way to end his troubles is to

> end his life, and thus formulate an intention to kill himself. As if in imitation of Samson, he decides to do so, let's say, by making the unsound structure he's living in come crashing down on him. As luck would have it, though, his new-born intention causes him to be so elated that he vigorously, joyously, and excitedly throws his arms over his head. . . . You guessed it: his arm strikes the wall; the building's rotted understructure gives way, and shortly thereafter, at the time specified (even if vaguely) in his intention, the building does indeed come crashing down, his death thereby resulting.[12]

The present analysis of suicide erroneously classes this as a case of suicide and is therefore too wide. The problem here, according to Wreen, concerns "deviant causal chains": "Somehow the causal journey from intention to action goes astray, even though it does arrive at its final destination on time, and even though it passes through one or more of the byways that it should."[13]

Wreen argues that since deviant causal chains are called deviant because they deviate from the agent's "action-plan" ("his plan of interlinked and generated actions leading up to his would-be intentional action"[14]), a further condition is necessary:

(4)   The causal route from the intention specified in (1) to the action described in (2) is more or less in accordance with S's action-plan.

Why not demand that the causal route from intention to action be in perfect agreement with the agent's action-plan? Although Wreen does not consider this question explicitly, such a requirement would render the analysis too narrow, for we are prepared to call an act a case of suicide even when the actual course of events does not transpire exactly as the agent planned. The following case helps make this point:

Case G:

> Gottlob has decided to kill himself by shooting himself in the mouth, but when the occasion arises

his hand trembles so much that he shoots himself in
the neck, thereby causing his death.[15]

Clearly, Gottlob has committed suicide, even though the actual
course of events deviated somewhat from the course specified in his
action-plan. Therefore, we cannot demand that the actual course of
events leading to the agent's death exactly mirror the course
specified in his action-plan. Such a move would leave us with an
unacceptably narrow analysis of suicide. This seems to be a defect
in Glenn Graber's definition of suicide, part of which claims that
suicide is "doing something that results in one's death *in the way
that was planned*."[16]

Of course, the present analysis still contains the rather
vague requirement that the actual course of events "more or less"
follow the agent's action-plan. I do not intend to pursue the problem
of specifying exactly what degree of conformity between the agent's
action-plan and the actual course of events is required. Any hard
and fast cut-off point is bound to be arbitrary. However, this does
not mean that the distinction between suicidal and non-suicidal acts
of self-killing is useless or illusory. Any hard and fast distinction
between purple and pink is bound to be arbitrary, but this does not
render the purple/pink distinction useless or illusory. The same
holds for the suicide/non-suicide distinction.

Have we reached anything like a satisfactory analysis of
suicide? Wreen claims that we still need a further condition:

(5)   S acts voluntarily in killing himself.

The reason for this addition is that (1)-(4) could be satisfied by the
following case, which Wreen claims is not a case of suicide:

Case H:

> . . . unbeknownst to him, [Harry] has electrodes
> implanted in his brain, and some of his intentions
> and beliefs, and not just his actions, have been
> programmed into him by--him again--a mad scientist.
> [He is] programmed to satisfy (1)-(4).[17]

It seems to me that Wreen is correct in claiming that Case H is not a case of suicide and in requiring that the agent act voluntarily. Since this may not be immediately obvious, perhaps the point can be made by altering Case H somewhat. Suppose that Harry knows that his mind is about to come under the control of the evil scientist. The scientist tells him of the experiment and of his plan to tamper with his intentions so that he kills himself. Before the scientist tampers with Harry's intentions, Harry begs the scientist to spare him. Naturally, his pleas are contemptuously dismissed as the scientist pulls the lever which sends Harry on the way to satisfying conditions (1)-(4). This example does not seem to be a case of suicide, and the reason why it is not a suicide is that Harry's act was not voluntary; his action was not strictly "up to him."

So far, following Wreen's lead, we have the following account:

Person S commits suicide at time T if and only if:

(1)   S intends at T to kill himself,

(2)   S acts at T in such a way as to kill himself,

(3)   the intention specified in (1) causes (via a number of generated actions) the action described in (2),

(4)   the causal route from the intention specified in (1) to the action described in (2) is more or less in accordance with S's action-plan, and

(5)   S acts voluntarily in killing himself.

I will now try to show how this analysis must be modified and qualified and how it is to be properly interpreted. Afterwards, some objections against Intentional Analyses in general will be considered.

Wreen contends that condition (1) must be modified. The intention to kill oneself must have a "strong desire" aspect; the agent must have a strong desire to kill himself. For Wreen, the kind of desire in question must be "a strong, or relatively strong, covetous state."[18] To illustrate the distinction between strong or relatively strong desires and weak or relatively weak desires, Wreen claims that

> a starving man's desire-at-t to eat-at-t is a strong, or relatively strong, covetous state, while many of his other desires-at-t, such as his desire-to-talk-to-his-wife-at-t, are weak, or relatively weak--meaning low on an "absolute scale" of desire-intensity, or relatively low on a list which ranks his desires by intensity.[19]

It seems to me that here we must part company with Wreen. This requirement would make the analysis of suicide too narrow. In order to show this, we can begin by considering some of the kinds of cases which Wreen is led to class as instances of non-suicidal self-killing:

Case I:

> Immanuel, a convicted prisoner, does what the executioner should do, and commutes, with his own hand, a painful death to one that is painless.

Case J:

> Jerry, an astronaut, takes a tablet in order to kill himself after being told that his spacecraft is doomed.

Case K:

> Karen, an amateur parachutist whose chute won't open, spares herself sixty seconds of terror by shooting herself in mid-fall.

"With each," says Wreen, "the pre-theoretical judgment is: self-killing, yes; suicide, no."[20]

Wreen's claim that these are not cases of suicide seems to run against the grain of "pre-theoretical" intuition. Cases I, J, and K, it seems, are cases of suicide. No one would doubt that these were

cases of suicide unless she were already committed to some special--
and mistaken--analysis of suicide.

Wreen is sympathetic to this objection. He claims that if we
do classify these cases as suicides, it is because we believe that they
involve the strong desire mentioned above.[21] This is implausible.
Even when we add that Immanuel, Jerry, and Karen did not have
a strong desire to kill themselves, this does not alter the judgment
that they committed suicide. Thus, Wreen's claim that suicide
essentially involves a strong desire to kill oneself seems mistaken.

Another way to see this is to consider "insurance money
suicides," cases in which someone arranges her own "accidental"
death so that her family can collect insurance money. Wreen is
forced to claim that in such suicides there is a strong desire on the
part of the agent to kill herself.[22] But surely we must admit the
possibility that some insurance money suicides desire to kill
themselves no more than Immanuel, Jones, or Karen and no more
than the bankrupt executive who shoots herself. If so, then once
again we have seen reason to give up Wreen's strong desire
condition.

Some philosophers who accept an Intentional Analysis of
suicide have claimed that the intention must be directed exclusively
at self-destruction, or at least that self-destruction must be the
agent's overriding concern. Thus, according to Joseph Margolis,
suicide is the deliberate taking of one's life simply in order to end it,
not instrumentally for any ulterior purpose. Later he weakens this
somewhat; we are told that the suicide's "*overriding* concern is to
end his own life, not for the sake of any independent objective."[23]
Likewise, Terence O'Keeffe suggests that the suicide "kills himself
for no other reason than to terminate his life." In fact, his motives
must involve "hatred of self, of the world, of existence itself."[24]
According to these accounts, then, one commits suicide only if one's
overriding intention is self-destruction.

One problem with this requirement is that it rules out
"altruistic suicides." Although some philosophers have been hesitant
to accept the possibility of altruistic suicide,[25] there seem to be clear
cases in which a person commits suicide even though his overriding
intention is altruistic. The insurance money suicides considered
earlier provide us with one kind of example.[26] In such cases, the
agent's overriding intention may be to relieve others. Nevertheless,
they are suicides. Another example is provided by R.F. Holland, who

seems to admit the possibility of altruistic suicide, but only very reluctantly:

Case L:

> [Larry] suffers and knows that he suffers from a congenital form of mental instability, as a result of which he is overtaken from time to time by irresistible impulses towards something very horrible, such as raping children. Getting himself locked up is no solution, either because no one will listen to him or because no mental hospital is secure enough to contain him during one of his fits; and his fits come upon him without warning. So he decides to kill himself. [He succeeds.][27]

Clearly, Larry has committed suicide, though his overriding intention may well have been altruistic. Thus, when condition (1) states that the agent must intend to kill himself, this does not entail that self-destruction is his overriding aim, and it certainly does not entail that self-destruction is his exclusive aim. As our examples have illustrated, one can commit suicide even though one's overriding intention in killing oneself is altruistic in character. In suicide, one can intend one's death either as a means or as an end.[28]

Joseph Kupfer is another philosopher who would claim that the present analysis of suicide requires modification: in order for an act to be suicide,

> the agent must have the option of a rather indeterminate period of life. . . . The difference between foregoing a day and giving up twenty years is significant. . . . Strictly speaking, it is a matter of belief concerning the amount of time to live. An individual who expects to live quite a while but wouldn't (because of an unforeseen, impending disaster or affliction, for example) is still committing suicide. And someone who mistakenly believes that his death is imminent is, nonetheless, not a suicide.[29]

Kupfer, then, would modify the present analysis by adding a further condition:

(6)   S believes that he has the option of a rather indeterminate period of life.

      This requirement would also seem to render the analysis of suicide too narrow. Here we can point to the real-life suicide of Hermann Goering. Goering "cheated the hangman. Two hours before his turn would have come he swallowed a vial of poison that had been smuggled into his cell." Like his Fuehrer, "he had succeeded at the last hour in choosing the way in which he would depart this earth."[30] Goering believed that he was to be hanged and thereby killed in a few hours. Nevertheless, he committed suicide. Therefore, condition (6) would render the present analysis too narrow.
      So far, we have not found it necessary to modify the analysis under consideration. However, it seems desirable to rewrite the analysis in a way that will allow for the possibility of other-inflicted suicides. The present analysis may suggest that there can be no such thing as other-inflicted suicide. However, R.G. Frey has argued convincingly that there can be other-inflicted suicides.[31] Consider the following cases:

Case M:

> [Mark] . . . seriously wants to end it all. . . . To ensure success . . . he devises a plan: he begins to goad and taunt, to ridicule and humiliate his wife, whom he knows to be of an exceedingly nervous, fragile temperament; and over many weeks his goading, etc., supplemented by beatings, reach fever pitch. . . . In a passion, she kills [him].

Case N:

> [Ned] wants to end it all. He . . . devises a plan by which someone else kills him. He purchases a gun and blanks and then threatens to kill his small son. When the police arrive, he releases his son and dashes into a neighboring warehouse, . . . hides

> behind a large crate, waiting for one of the policemen
> to come in after him. . . . When this happens, [Ned]
> jumps out from behind the crate, yells an obscenity,
> waits for the policeman to turn, and then fires one of
> his blanks. The policeman whirls round, comes face
> to face with [Ned's] gun, and instinctively squeezes
> off his own. . . . [Ned] is killed.[32]

Cases M and N both seem to me to be cases of suicide. This claim raises two concerns. First, it might be said that M and N are cases of murder or manslaughter by another party. But this claim need not conflict with the claim that they are cases of suicide. If Frey is right in contending that Cases M and N fall into the category of other-inflicted suicide, and if we insist that these are cases of murder or manslaughter by another party, we will be compelled to admit that there are exceptions to the assumption that one and the same death cannot be an instance of both suicide and murder or manslaughter by another party.[33] This assumption, however, is based partly on the assumption that Frey is challenging: namely, that other-inflicted suicide is impossible. Further, as Frey has put it, "if one can be a suicide and be killed by a train . . . , why can one not be a suicide and be killed by another person?"[34]

The second worry concerns whether or not we need to add a further condition to our analysis. Some may doubt that an other-inflicted death should count as suicide when the victim was uncertain in his predictions concerning the killer's actions. For example, some may feel unsure as to whether Case M is a case of suicide since the victim may not have been certain about his wife's behavior. Do we need to add that, in the case of other-inflicted suicide, the suicide must have some relatively high degree of certainty about the actions of the other party or parties involved?

My own suspicion is that we do not. Even if the suicide were relatively uncertain about the reactions of the other party or parties involved, he might still have committed suicide, it seems to me, if the actions of the other party or parties involved were (more or less) in agreement with his action-plan. Suppose, for example, that Mark (Case M) was actually quite bad at predicting his wife's behavior but that his action-plan, which involved his wife's killing him, was realized for some bizarre reason. I am inclined to say that he has committed suicide. It seems to me that so long as his wife acted in the manner specified (however vaguely) in his action-plan, he committed suicide. However, I admit that this may not harmonize with everyone's intuitions. Since nothing of great importance is at stake, readers who think that some kind of certainty requirement needs to be added when we consider cases of other-inflicted suicide are invited to add such a condition. However, in the future I will not mention such a condition.

Since, then, there can be other-inflicted suicides, what is essential in suicide is that the agent arrange her own death, not that she kill herself. With this in mind, we should rewrite conditions (1), (2), and (5) of the present analysis as follows:

(1)   S intends at T to bring about his own death,

(2)   S acts at T in such a way as to bring about his own death,

(5)   S acts voluntarily in bringing about his own death.

When I say that S "brings about" his own death, what I mean is that S either kills himself (e.g., he fatally shoots himself in the head) or he places himself in circumstances which kill him (e.g., he refuses to budge from subway tracks just as a train is speeding towards him). This is meant to cover cases of other-inflicted suicide. It is important to note that when condition (1), for example, reads: "S intends at T to bring about his own death," the phrase "bring about" does not abbreviate "intentionally brings about" or anything of the sort, for then condition (1) would be an abbreviated way of saying: "S intends at T to intentionally bring about his own death." "Brings about," as I here use the phrase, is not to be defined by reference to intentions. In my sense of the phrase, Al (Case A) brought about his own death.

However, as Tolhurst has shown by the following example, one need not arrange *all* the events in the external world which cause one's own death in order to commit suicide:

Case O:

> [O'Brien] has decided that his life is no longer worth living and proposes to end it all by jumping into a nearby ravine. However, on the way to the ravine he

finds himself about to be engulfed by an avalanche
which he could avoid without much difficulty.
Nonetheless he allows himself to be killed by the
avalanche and thus saves the trouble of walking to
the ravine.[35]

According to Tolhurst, O'Brien has committed suicide even though
he was killed by conditions which he did not completely arrange in
order to bring about his own death. I agree that this is a case of
suicide. It may be thought that this conflicts with my requirement
that the suicide must bring about his own death. But there is no
conflict. The reason is that Tolhurst's example disposes only of the
following claim: an agent did not commit suicide if he died by taking
advantage of events in his surroundings which he did not create to
bring about his own death. I am not defending that claim. Like
Tolhurst, I reject it. With regard to the case at hand, the only sense
in which O'Brien did not bring about his own death is that he did
not bring about the avalanche. But when I claim that the suicide
brings about his own death, I mean to include cases where he takes
advantage of his surroundings in order to cause his own death. On
the ordinary (and my) sense of the phrase "bring about," O'Brien has
clearly brought about his own death, even though he did not bring
about the avalanche.

    Some proponents of Intentional Analyses claim that lack of
"coercion" is a necessary condition for suicide.[36] If this means no
more than that voluntariness is a necessary condition for suicide,
then we have already accepted their claim. However, it seems that
their claim may not be the same as the claim that voluntariness is
a necessary condition for suicide. The term "coerced," as used by
these writers and their critics, may mean something like "pressured
by others," such as one's friends or relatives.[37] In this sense, one can
do something under coercion and yet do it voluntarily since an act
can still be strictly "up to me" in the sense that I willed it and my
volitions were not under the control of another entity (e.g., an evil
scientist) even though I did the act under pressure from others;
doing something under pressure from others is not analogous to
doing it because one's will is completely controlled by an outside
force, such as our evil scientist. On the present meaning of "coerce,"
a teenager's parents may pressure him to go to college and thereby
coerce him into going, but if he goes, it does not follow that he went

involuntarily, for he had control over his own will. There is a distinction between an involuntary act, such as the act of a person whose brain is under the control of an evil scientist, and a merely coerced act in the sense of "coerced" that seems to be used by these writers. For an act can be coerced in the sense that it was done under pressure from other people but yet be voluntary in the sense that the agent's will was not controlled by external factors. Although we do speak of "forcing" people by means of threats, this does not mean that the agent's will is under the complete control of another person. In ordinary life we might say that the teenager whose parents coerced him into going to college went involuntarily, but strictly speaking we can make a distinction between the involuntary and the merely coerced. A person whose mental states are controlled by an evil scientist acts involuntarily when the scientist tampers with his mental states in such a way as to produce a certain act. On the other hand, if someone is merely "forced" to do something by means of threats, he acts under mere coercion but not involuntarily. The teenager whose parents "force" him to go to college is in a position to simply refuse to go; the man whose brain is being manipulated by an evil scientist is not in a position to simply refuse cooperation.

If the claim that lack of coercion is a necessary condition for suicide means simply that absence of any "pressure" from others is a necessary condition for suicide, then the claim seems dubious. As Tolhurst has noted, "Japanese literature abounds with stories of samurai who are pressured into committing *seppuku*, ritual disembowelment." Since it "seems plausible to suppose that anyone who commits *seppuku* commits suicide," and since people can be and have been pressured into committing *seppuku*, "it is reasonable to conclude that coerced suicide is possible."[38] Further, Tolhurst asks us to consider a case where a man is a prisoner of a sadistic tyrant who wants him to kill himself and who informs him that if he does not do so he will be tortured to death in the most horrific way imaginable. In order to avoid a long and agonizing death, he shoots himself. Here we have a clear case of coerced (i.e., "pressured") self-killing. (Nevertheless, the prisoner acted voluntarily; the sadistic tyrant did not have strict control over his will; he, like the teenager who goes to college under parental threats, is in a position to simply refuse cooperation.) But it also seems to be a case of suicide, for it does not differ in any relevant way from the case of suicide in which a soldier, knowing that he is about to be captured by enemies who will torture him to death merely for their own amusement, shoots himself to avoid a long and agonizing death.[39] It seems, then, that we must allow for the possibility of coerced (i.e., "pressured") suicide.

I now want to consider some objections which have been raised against Intentional Analyses of suicide in general. These are directed against any Intentional Analysis, not merely the one endorsed and elaborated here. First I will consider Durkheim's objections. Afterwards, I will consider another argument for the claim that the intention to bring about one's death is not a necessary condition for suicide. Finally, a more general criticism will be discussed.

Durkheim offers two criticisms of Intentional Analyses. First, he argues that to define the concept of suicide in terms of the suicide's intentions is to appeal to a characteristic which, "whatever its interest and significance, would at least suffer from not being easily recognizable, since it is not easily observed."[40]

Durkheim is certainly right in claiming that it is not always easy or even possible to infer someone's intentions from his observed behavior. However, this does not show that the concept of suicide can be adequately analyzed without reference to the suicide's intentions. All it succeeds in showing, for the supporter of Intentional Analyses, is that it is not always easy to know whether or not someone has committed suicide. But there is nothing at all surprising in this implication. For precisely what we find is that it is often unclear whether or not someone has committed suicide. For example, if an individual who is suspected of having committed suicide did not leave a suicide note and died because of a slight overdose of prescribed medication, it may not be clear whether or not we have a case of suicide or accidental death. So there is nothing unusual in the conclusion which Durkheim derives from Intentional Analyses. Any account which made it all too easy to decide whether or not a person has committed suicide would thereby merit suspicion.

A second Durkheimian objection claims that

> if the intention of self-destruction alone constituted suicide, the name suicide could not be given to facts which, despite apparent differences, are fundamentally identical with those always called suicide. . . . The soldier facing certain death to save

> his regiment does not wish to die, and yet is he not
> as much the author of his own death as the
> manufacturer or merchant who kills himself to avoid
> bankruptcy?[41]

Durkheim claims that the soldier's act is suicide despite the fact that he did not wish to die. This is thought to show that the concept of suicide cannot be analyzed in terms of intentions.

There seem to be two mistakes in this claim. First, Durkheim mistakenly identifies wishing with intending. One can wish that some state of affairs obtain (e.g, the death of one's spouse) without intending to bring it about, and one can intend to do something (e.g., go to the dentist to undergo a painful procedure) without wishing to do it. A second problem with Durkheim's claim is that it is simply counterintuitive to say that anyone who, like the soldier, knowingly does something that will lead to his own death thereby commits suicide. Consider the analogous case mentioned earlier (Case D) of a doctor who treats plague victims knowing that she will die as a result. Like the case of the soldier facing certain death, this case involves someone who knows that what she is doing will lead to her death. Nevertheless, the doctor has not committed suicide. Likewise, one can face certain death in battle without thereby committing suicide.

Durkheim's objections fail to dispose of Intentional Analyses, but it must be said in all fairness that Durkheim's ends were not the same as those of the present inquiry. What he wanted was the most useful definition of "suicide" from the standpoint of sociological inquiry. While he did not define "suicide" solely in behavioristic terms, he regarded his definition in terms of the agent's knowledge as giving an account that would make suicide relatively easy to detect, for it is generally easier, according to Durkheim, to infer someone's knowledge than it is to infer his intentions.[42] Durkheim explicitly stated that

> we shall combine under that name [i.e., "suicide"]
> absolutely all the facts presenting these distinctive
> characteristics, regardless of whether the resulting
> class fails to include all cases ordinarily included
> under the name or includes others usually otherwise
> classified. The essential thing is not to express . . .

what the average intelligence terms suicide, but to
establish a category of objects permitting this
classification, which are objectively established. . . .[43]

From the standpoint of the social sciences, then, it may be
that a more verifiable definition of "suicide" is desirable, one that
does not refer to the suicide's intentions, just as psychologists
frequently find it desirable to give "operational definitions" of
mentalistic terms like "intelligence" in order to render their research
possible. From the standpoint of social science research, perhaps
Durkheim's definition is more useful than Intentional Analyses while
doing less violence to the ordinary concept of suicide than, say, the
Self-Killing Analysis.[44] However, our present concern is not to find
the most useful analysis of suicide from the perspective of empirical
inquiry. We must, then, leave both Durkheim's definition of "suicide"
and his objections to Intentional Analyses behind.

Peter Windt and others have argued that all Intentional
Analyses of suicide are defective because one can commit suicide
even though one has not intended one's own death. This, we are told,
can be shown by the existence of "compulsive suicides":[45]

Case P:

> [Pablo] has been suffering for some time from a
> recurring compulsion to commit suicide. He fears
> this compulsion, desires not to succumb to it, has
> sought aid in combatting it, but it grows in him as
> he hikes [one] day, and at [a] bridge it drives him
> into the water and to his death.[46]

Windt claims that this counts as a case of suicide and that "the very
nature of the compulsion and his struggle with it indicates that he
did not desire to die nor intend to do so."[47]

This claim raises two problems. First, it is not completely
clear that Pablo has in fact committed suicide since it is unclear
whether or not he killed himself voluntarily.[48] As we saw earlier, the
concept of suicide presupposes that the agent acted voluntarily in
bringing about his own death. However, since Windt does not discuss
the nature of the compulsion in question, it seems desirable to
stipulate, merely for the sake of argument, that the kind of

compulsion which drove Pablo over the side of the bridge was not such that his killing himself was involuntary. Perhaps it was merely a relatively strong temptation.

This still leaves us with a second problem. Windt argues as follows: (i) Pablo struggled against his compulsion to kill himself; therefore, (ii) he neither desired to kill himself nor intended to do so. But (ii) does not follow from (i). From the fact that he struggled against his compulsion to kill himself it does not follow that he did not desire to kill himself. Nor does it follow that he did not intend to kill himself. Perhaps he had conflicting desires and conflicting intentions. First, presumably his compulsion was itself a compulsive *desire* to kill himself. If so, then he did desire to kill himself, even though he also may have had a desire not to kill himself, as is shown by his struggle against his compulsion. There is nothing incoherent in this idea. Just as people often believe a proposition and its contradictory and thereby fall into inconsistency, so they sometimes have a desire that a certain state of affairs obtain while also having a desire that the very same state of affairs not obtain. They are then said to have conflicting desires. Second, as for Pablo's intentions, the same can be said. Even if we agree that he had an intention not to kill himself, it does not follow that he did not also have an intention to kill himself. Just as our beliefs can be inconsistent and our desires in conflict, so our intentions may be in conflict. Admittedly, this seems to occur less frequently than the analogous circumstances in the case of belief and desire. But the compulsive neurotic who struggles against performing the acts which his compulsion drives him towards seems to be one kind of case where the agent's intentions may be in conflict. The compulsive hand-washer, for instance, has the intention to wash his hands, but his desire to fight his affliction together with his beliefs about ways of refraining from performing the act may give birth to an intention to refrain from washing his hands. I conclude, then, that compulsive suicide examples like Windt's do not establish that there can be suicide even when the agent does not intend his own death.

Perhaps it will be said that Intentional Analyses in general, and the present analysis in particular, are unacceptable because they analyze the concept of suicide in terms of other concepts which are themselves problematic. After all, the present analysis and others like it analyze suicide in terms of such problematic concepts as intentional action, voluntary behavior, causality, and so on. These concepts are themselves part of the landscape of philosophy's battlefields.

It is undeniable that Intentional Analyses define "suicide" in terms of other concepts which are themselves subject to dispute. What this shows is that the concept of suicide is more problematic than we might initially have thought. It does not follow from the fact that our analysis makes the concept of suicide dependent on other problematic concepts that it is mistaken. Precisely the same phenomenon can be found in other areas of philosophy. Epistemologists, for example, have served up an unbelievably large heap of analyses of the concept of knowledge, but all involve some concept or other which is an object of philosophical dispute. This fact in itself, however, is not taken as evidence that any such analysis is incorrect. Likewise, if Intentional Analyses involve other problematic concepts, this in itself does not show that they are mistaken.

No discussion of the concept of suicide would be complete without considering the most controversial case in the literature on the subject. While some frequently mentioned difficult cases have already been discussed, I must briefly deal with the case of Socrates.

Frey, who accepts an Intentional Analysis, claims that Socrates committed suicide. He drank the hemlock knowingly, "not unknowingly or in ignorance of what its effect on him would be, and intentionally, not accidentally or mistakenly," and "he died as a result of his act of drinking the hemlock."[49]

Since several philosophers have doubted or denied that Socrates committed suicide,[50] our analysis would indeed be suspicious if it yielded a very easy answer to the question of whether or not he committed suicide. In fact, our analysis does not hand down an easy verdict, despite Frey's claims. For from the fact that Socrates intentionally drank the hemlock which he knew would kill him, it does not follow that he intended to bring about his own death. One can intend to perform an action, know that it has a certain consequence, and yet not intend that consequence, as the following example illustrates:

> suppose Monica attends a lecture in which she learns that the movement of largish physical objects causes the movement of air molecules. Does that entail that when she walks out of the lecture and

drives home, Monica is moving air molecules intentionally? It seems obvious that she does not.[51]

Similarly, although I know that by brushing my teeth I am wearing out my toothbrush, and although I intentionally brush my teeth, it does not follow that I intentionally wear out my toothbrush. This is an unintended but foreseen side-effect of intentionally brushing my teeth. Finally, I may knowingly increase the profits of the Coca-Cola Corporation by intentionally buying a Coke, but it does not follow that part of my intention is to increase the profits of the Coca-Cola Corporation.[52]

But Frey is aware of this possible reply to his argument:

> one might argue . . . that though he foresaw as a consequence of drinking the hemlock (as his sentence) that he would die, what he wanted was not to die but to uphold the laws of Athens. It is equally plausible to argue, however, that Socrates wanted to die, sentenced, as he was, by the city to do so, in order to uphold--and be seen upholding--these very laws.[53]

According to Frey, then, it is "equally plausible" to think that Socrates did intend to bring about his own death. But, of course, this would not show that he did in fact intend to bring about his own death. In fact, it points out exactly why the case of Socrates is so controversial. We cannot give any *conclusive* reason for thinking that Socrates intended to bring about his own death, for his intention may have been something like "I will fulfil my political obligations at all cost, even death" rather than "I will kill myself in order to fulfil my political obligations." In the former case, his own death is merely a foreseen but unintended consequence, while in the latter his own death is intended. Even if Socrates frequently expressed a desire to die, it still does not follow that he intended to kill himself. For it might still be the case that killing himself was not part of his intention on the occasion of his death. Similarly, even if (i) I frequently want to wear down my toothbrush, (ii) I intentionally brush my teeth, and (iii) I know that this will wear down my toothbrush, it does not follow that I intentionally wear down my toothbrush, for perhaps wearing down my toothbrush is not, *on this occasion*, part of my reason for acting as I do; it is not part of my intention *in this instance*. On this occasion, my desire to wear down my toothbrush--a desire which, for some odd reason, I frequently have--does not form part of my reason for brushing.

My approach, then, to the case of Socrates is to say that we cannot give *conclusive* reasons for preferring one of the following interpretations of his action over the other:

(A)   Socrates intended his own death. (E.g., "I am going to kill myself in order to fulfill my duty.")

(B)   Socrates did not intend his own death, but merely foresaw that it would result from his actions. (E.g., "I am going to do my duty no matter what, even if I die.")

On the present analysis, we are forced to say that Socrates committed suicide only if we accept claim (A). But since it seems difficult to justify certainty in preferring (A) over (B), I do not think we can settle the enigma of Socrates's death in a conclusive way. However, unlike some philosophers, I have no pressing need or desire to deny that Socrates committed suicide. In fact, I suspect that (A) is the case given Socrates's frequently expressed positive estimations of the value of death, even though, as admitted above, Socrates's frequently stated desire to die does not *entail* that (A) is the case. Given the ethical views defended in this work, the fact that he committed suicide, if it is a fact, does not in itself detract from his image as a moral hero.

Perhaps it will be thought that Socrates did not kill himself voluntarily and is therefore not a suicide since, as we have seen, voluntariness is a necessary condition for suicide. But according to Frey, Socrates

> did not drink the hemlock against his will: his jailers
> were not required to . . . hold him down and pour the
> hemlock down his throat. Even granted that he had
> to die, Socrates had a choice between drinking the
> hemlock willingly and having it . . . force-fed. . . . I
> deny that intentionally taking one's life because it is
> one's sentence *ipso facto* precludes committing
> suicide. Suppose that the sentence for murder was a

bit different, that every convicted murderer was allowed to live for twelve months . . . , and could either take his own life within this period or else face the absolute certainty of a state execution at the end of the twelve months: do not the murderers who intentionally take their own lives commit suicide?[54]

Socrates was certainly "pressured" to kill himself, but I agree with Frey that his act was nevertheless voluntary; his case is like that of the teenager who is pressured to go to college by his parents, not like that of the man whose mental states are under the complete control of an evil scientist. Socrates was in a position to simply refuse to cooperate. He was in a position to say, "If you want me dead you're going to have to hold me down and pour that stuff down my throat." This he did not do.

Conclusion

It will be useful to conclude with a summary statement of the revised Wreenian analysis of suicide defended in this appendix:

Person S commits suicide at time T if and only if:

(1)   S intends at T to bring about his own death,

(2)   S acts at T in such a way as to bring about his own death,

(3)   the intention specified in (1) causes (through a number of generated actions) the action described in (2),

(4)   the causal route from the intention specified in (1) to the action described in (2) is more or less in accordance with S's action-plan, and

(5)   S acts voluntarily in bringing about his own death.

Admittedly, this definition is not as precise as one might like. For example, condition (4) requires that the causal route from intention to action be "more or less" in accordance with the agent's action plan. Nor will everyone find this account acceptable. However, for the reasons given at the beginning of this appendix, it is unlikely in the extreme that any analysis of suicide will ever become universally received or that there is an analysis which is both plausible and perfectly precise.

Notes

1. Paul Edwards ed. *The Encyclopedia of Philosophy* (New York: Free Press, 1967), s.v. "Suicide," by Glanville Williams.

2. Harry Lesser, "Suicide and Self-Murder," *Philosophy* 55 (1980): 255.

3. Emile Durkheim, *Suicide*, trans. John A. Spaulding and George Simpson (Glencoe: Free Press, 1951), 44.

4. William E. Tolhurst, "Suicide, Self-Sacrifice, and Coercion," in *Suicide: Right or Wrong?*, ed. John Donnelly (Buffalo: Prometheus Books, 1990), 80.

5. Terence M. O'Keeffe, "Suicide and Self-Starvation," in *Suicide: Right or Wrong?*, ed. John Donnelly, 123.

6. James W. McGray, "Bobby Sands, Suicide, and Self-Sacrifice," *Journal of Value Inquiry* 17 (1983): 67. For other examples, see Tolhurst, "Suicide," 79; and two other articles in *Suicide: Right or Wrong?*, ed. John Donnelly: Suzanne Stern-Gillet, "The Rhetoric of Suicide," 95; Glen C. Graber, "Mastering the Concept of Suicide," 137.

7. R.F. Holland, *Against Empiricism* (Oxford: Basil Blackwell, 1980), 144.

8. Michael Wreen, "The Definition of Suicide," *Social Theory and Practice* 14 (1988): 1-23.

9. Ibid., 5-6; for more on the problem of deviant causal chains, see Tolhurst, "Suicide," 89-90.

10. Alvin Goldman, *A Theory of Human Action* (Princeton: Princeton University Press, 1970), 20-48.

11. Ibid., 21-27.

12. Wreen, "The Definition of Suicide," 5-6.

13. Ibid., 6.

14. Ibid. This terminology is also derived from Alvin Goldman: "The combination of an agent's action-*wants* and his *projected act-tree* I shall call an *action-plan*"; "projected act trees . . represent hypothetical acts that the agent . . . *believes* would be performed *if* S were to perform a certain basic act." Goldman, *A Theory of Human Action*, 56.

15. Adapted from Tolhurst, "Suicide," 90.

16. Graber, "Mastering the Concept of Suicide," 141, emphasis added.

17. Wreen, "The Definition of Suicide," 7.

18. Ibid., 7.

19. Ibid.

20. Ibid., 16.

21. Ibid., 22, note 38.

22. Ibid., 10.

23. Joseph Margolis, *Negativities: The Limits of Life* (Columbus: Charles E. Merrill Publishing Co., 1975), 26-27, emphasis added.

24. O'Keeffe, "Suicide and Self-Starvation," 132.

25. E.g., Holland, *Against Empiricism*, 149, 152.

26. See Tolhurst, "Suicide," 81; Tom L. Beauchamp, "What Is Suicide?," in *Ethical Issues in Death and Dying*, ed. Robert F. Weir (New York: Columbia University Press, 1986), 324.

27. Holland, *Against Empiricism*, 149-50.

28. See Tolhurst, "Suicide," 85-89; Milton A. Gonsalves, "Theistic and Nontheistic Arguments," in *Suicide: Right or Wrong?*, ed. John Donnelly, 179; Graber, "Mastering the Concept of Suicide," 141.

29. Joseph Kupfer, "Suicide: Its Nature and Moral Evaluation," *Journal of Value Inquiry* 24 (1990): 68.

30. William L. Shirer, *The Rise and Fall of the Third Reich* (New York: Simon and Schuster, 1960), 1143.

31. R.G. Frey, "Suicide and Self-Inflicted Death," in *Suicide: Right or Wrong?*, ed. John Donnelly.

32. Both examples adapted from Frey, ibid., 112-13.

33. Ibid., 115.

34. Ibid., 112.

35. Tolhurst, "Suicide," 82.

36. Beauchamp, "What Is Suicide?," 328.

37. Tolhurst, "Suicide," 83.

38. Ibid.

39. Ibid., 84.

40. Durkheim, *Suicide*, 43.

41. Ibid.

42. Ibid., 44. This claim, of course, is open to doubt.

43. Ibid., 42.

44. However, see Maurice L. Farber, *Theory of Suicide* (New York: Funk & Wagnalls, 1968), Chapter 1.

45. Peter Y. Windt, "The Concept of Suicide," in *Suicide: The Philosophical Issues*, ed. M.P. Battin and D.J. Mayo (London: Peter Owen, 1980), 42-43; Jack Douglas, *The Social Meanings of Suicide* (Princeton: Princeton University Press, 1967), 356-59.

46. Windt, "The Concept of Suicide," 42.

47. Ibid., 42-43.

48. Wreen, "The Definition of Suicide," 17.

49. R.G. Frey, "Did Socrates Commit Suicide?," in *Suicide: The Philosophical Issues*, ed. M.P. Battin and D.J. Mayo, 36.

50. E.g., Holland, *Against Empiricism*, 146; R.A. Duff, "Socratic Suicide?," *Proceedings of the Aristotelian Society* 83 (1982-83): 35-48; Wreen, "The Definition of Suicide," 14.

51. Michael Smith, "Did Socrates Kill Himself Intentionally?," *Philosophy* 55 (1980): 253.

52. For this kind of reply to Frey, see Duff, "Socratic Suicide," 36. Also Kupfer, "Suicide," 70; and Tolhurst, "Suicide," 85, who authored the Coke example.

53. Frey, "Did Socrates Commit Suicide?," 36.

54. Ibid., 36-37.

BIBLIOGRAPHY

Alvarez, A. *The Savage God: A Study of Suicide*. New York: Random House, 1970.

Amundsen, Darrel W. "Suicide and Early Christian Values." In *Suicide and Euthanasia: Historical and Contemporary Themes*, ed. Baruch A. Brody, 77-153. Dordrecht: Kluwer Academic Publishers, 1989.

Aquinas, St. Thomas. *Basic Writings of Saint Thomas Aquinas*. Edited by Anton C. Pegis. Vol. 2. New York: Random House, 1945.

------. "The Catholic View." In *Suicide: Right or Wrong?*, ed. John Donnelly, 33-36. Buffalo: Prometheus Books, 1990.

Aristotle. *Nicomachean Ethics*. Translated by W.D. Ross. In *The Basic Works of Aristotle*, ed. Richard McKeon. New York: Random House, 1941.

Augustine, St. *The City of God*. Translated by Marcus Dods. *Great Books of the Western World*. Edited by Robert Maynard Hutchins. Vol. 18. Chicago: Encyclopedia Britannica, Inc., 1952.

Baelz, P.R. "Suicide: Some Theological Reflections." In *Suicide: The Philosophical Issues*, ed. M.P. Battin and D.J. Mayo, 71-83. London: Peter Owen, 1980.

Barrington, Mary Rose. "Apologia for Suicide." In *Suicide: The Philosophical Issues*, ed. M.P. Battin and D.J. Mayo, 90-103. London: Peter Owen, 1980.

Battin, Margaret P. "Suicide: A Fundamental Human Right?" In *Suicide: The Philosophical Issues*, ed. M.P. Battin and D.J. Mayo, 267-85. London: Peter Owen, 1980.

------. *Ethical Issues in Suicide*. Englewood Cliffs: Prentice-Hall, 1982.

Battin, Margaret P. and D.J. Mayo, ed. *Suicide: The Philosophical Issues*. London: Peter Owen, 1980.

Beauchamp, Tom. "An Analysis of Hume's Essay 'On Suicide'." *Review of Metaphysics* 30 (September 1976): 73-95.

------. "Suicide." In *Matters of Life and Death*. 2nd ed., ed. Tom Regan. 77-124. Philadelphia: Temple University Press, 1986.

------. "What Is Suicide?" In *Ethical Issues in Death and Dying*, ed. Robert F. Weir. 323-29. New York: Columbia University Press, 1986.

------. "Suicide in the Age of Reason." In *Suicide and Euthanasia: Historical and Contemporary Themes*, ed. Baruch A. Brody, 183-219. Dordrecht: Kluwer Academic Publishers, 1989.

Bentham, Jeremy. *An Introduction to the Principles of Morals and Legislation*. In *The English Philosophers from Bacon to Mill*, ed. Edwin A. Burtt, 791-852. New York: Modern Library, 1939.

Brandt, Richard B. "The Morality and Rationality of Suicide." In *Suicide: Right or Wrong?*, ed. John Donnelly, 185-200. Buffalo: Prometheus Books, 1990.

Camus, Albert. *The Myth of Sisyphus and Other Essays*. Translated by Justin O'Brien. New York: Vintage Books, 1983.

Choron, J. *Suicide*. New York: Charles Scribner's Sons, 1972.

Cohen, Elliot D. "Paternalism That Does Not Restrict Individuality: Criteria and Applications." *Social Theory and Practice* 12 (1986): 309-35.

Cooper, John M. "Greek Philosophers and Euthanasia and Suicide." In *Suicide and Euthanasia: Historical and Contemporary Themes*, ed. Baruch A. Brody, 9-38. Dordrecht: Kluwer Academic Publishers, 1989.

Copleston, Frederick. *Aquinas*. Baltimore: Penguin Books, 1955.

------. *Arthur Schopenhauer: Philosopher of Pessimism*. London: Search Press, 1975.

Devine, Philip E. "On Choosing Death." In *Suicide: The Philosophical Issues*, ed. M.P. Battin and D.J. Mayo, 138-142. London: Peter Owen, 1980.

Donne, John. *Biathanatos*. Edited by M. Rudick and M.P. Battin. New York: Garland, 1982.

Donnelly, John, ed. *Suicide: Right or Wrong?* Buffalo: Prometheus Books, 1990.

Douglas, Jack. *The Social Meanings of Suicide*. Princeton: Princeton University Press, 1967.

Duff, R.A. "Socratic Suicide?" *Proceedings of the Aristotelian Society* 83 (1982): 35-48.

Durkheim, Emile. *Suicide*. Translated by John A. Spaulding and George Simpson. Glencoe: Free Press, 1951.

Edwards, Paul, ed. *The Encyclopedia of Philosophy*. New York: Free Press, 1967. S.v. "Suicide," by Glanville Williams.

Farber, Maurice L. *Theory of Suicide*. New York: Funk and Wagnalls, 1968.

Feldman, Fred. *Confrontations with the Reaper*. New York: Oxford University Press, 1992.

Fletcher, Joseph. "Attitudes Toward Suicide." In *Suicide: Right or Wrong?*, ed. John Donnelly, 61-73. Buffalo: Prometheus Books, 1990.

Fox, Michael. "Schopenhauer on Death, Suicide and Self-Renunciation." In *Schopenhauer: His Philosophical Achievement*, ed. Michael Fox, 147-70. Brighton, UK: Harvester Press, 1980.

Frey, R.G. "Did Socrates Commit Suicide?" In *Suicide: The Philosophical Issues*, ed. M.P. Battin and D.J. Mayo, 35-38. London: Peter Owen, 1980.

------. "Suicide and Self-Inflicted Death." In *Suicide: Right or Wrong?*, ed. John Donnelly, 105-16. Buffalo: Prometheus Books, 1990.

Gardiner, Patrick. *Schopenhauer*. Baltimore: Penguin Books, 1963.

Glass, Ronald. "The Contradictions in Kant's Examples." *Philosophical Studies* 22 (1971): 65-70.

Glover, Jonathan. *Causing Death and Saving Lives*. London: Penguin Books, 1977.

Goldman, Alan H. *Moral Knowledge*. London and New York: Routledge, 1988.

Goldman, Alvin. *A Theory of Human Action*. Princeton: Princeton University Press, 1970.

Gonsalves, Milton A. "Theistic and Nontheistic Arguments." In *Suicide: Right or Wrong?*, ed. John Donnelly, 179-84. Buffalo: Prometheus Books, 1990.

Graber, Glenn C. "Mastering the Concept of Suicide." In *Suicide: Right or Wrong?*, ed. John Donnelly, 135-49. Buffalo: Prometheus Books, 1990.

Hill, Thomas E. "Self-Regarding Suicide: A Modified Kantian View." *Suicide and Life-Threatening Behavior* 13 (Winter 1983): 254-275.

Holland, R.F. *Against Empiricism*. Oxford: Basil Blackwell, 1980.

Hume, David. "Of Suicide." In *Dialogues Concerning Natural Religion and the Posthumous Essays*, ed. Richard H. Popkin, 97-105. Indianapolis: Hackett, 1980.

Jacobs, Jerry. *The Moral Justification of Suicide*. Springfield: Charles C. Thomas, 1982.

Josephus, Flavius. *The Jewish War*. Translated by H. St. J. Thackeray. Vol. 2. London: William Heinemann Ltd., 1927.

Kant, Immanuel. *Critique of Practical Reason and Other Writings in Moral Philosophy*. Edited and translated by Lewis White Beck. Chicago: University of Chicago Press, 1949.

------. *Groundwork of the Metaphysic of Morals*. Edited and translated by H.J. Paton. New York: Harper Torchbooks, 1964.

------. "Duties Towards the Body in Regard to Life." In *Suicide: Right or Wrong?*, ed. John Donnelly, 47-55. Buffalo: Prometheus Books, 1990.

Kastenbaum, Robert. "Suicide as the Preferred Way of Death." In *Suicidology: Contemporary Developments*, ed. by Edwin S. Shneidman, 421-441. New York: Grune and Stratton, 1976.

Kemp, J. "Kant's Examples of the Categorical Imperative." In *Foundations of the Metaphysics of Morals with Critical Essays*, ed. R.P. Wolff. New York: Bobbs-Merrill, 1969.

Kluge, Eike-Henner W. *The Practice of Death*. New Haven: Yale University Press, 1975.

Kuitert, Harry. "Have Christians the Right to Kill Themselves? From Self-Murder to Self-Killing." In *Suicide and the Right to Die*, ed. J. Pohier and D. Mieth, 100-6. Edinburgh: T. and T. Clark, Ltd., 1985.

Kupfer, Joseph. "Suicide: Its Nature and Moral Evaluation." *Journal of Value Inquiry* 24 (1990): 67-81.

Landsberg, Paul-Louis. *The Moral Problem of Suicide*. Translated by C. Rowland. New York: Philosophical Library, 1953.

Lebacqz, Karen, and H. Tristram Engelhardt. "Suicide." In *Death, Dying, and Euthanasia*, ed. Dennis Horan and David Mall, 669-705. Frederick: Aletheia, 1980.

Lesser, Harry. "Suicide and Self-Murder." *Philosophy* 55 (1980): 255-57.

Lester, David. *Questions and Answers about Suicide*. Philadelphia: The Charles Press, Publishers, 1989.

Locke, John. *An Essay Concerning the True Original, Extent and End of Civil Government*. In *The English Philosophers from Bacon to Mill*, ed. Edwin A. Burtt, 403-504. New York: Modern Library, 1939.

Macklin, Ruth. "Refusal of Psychiatric Treatment: Autonomy, Competence, and Paternalism." In *Psychiatry and Ethics*, ed. R.B. Edwards, 331-40. Buffalo: Prometheus Books, 1992.

Margolis, Joseph. *Negativities: The Limits of Life*. Columbus: Charles E. Merrill Publishing Co, 1975.

Martin, Robert. "Suicide and False Desires." In *Suicide: The Philosophical Issues*, ed. M.P. Battin and D.J. Mayo, 144-150. London: Peter Owen, 1980.

Mayo, David J. "The Concept of Rational Suicide." *The Journal of Medicine and Philosophy* 11 (1986): 143-155.

McBride, Joseph. *Albert Camus: Philosopher and Litterateur*. New York: St. Martin's Press, 1992.

McCaughey, J.D. "Suicide: Some Theological Considerations." *Theology* 70 (February 1967): 63-68.

McGray, James W. "Bobby Sands, Suicide, and Self-Sacrifice." *Journal of Value Inquiry* 17 (1983): 65-75.

Montaigne, Michel Eyquem de. *The Essays*. Translated by Charles Cotton. *Great Books of the Western World*. Edited by Robert Maynard Hutchins. Vol. 25. Chicago: Encyclopedia Britannica, Inc., 1952.

Moreland, J.P., and Geisler, Norman L. *The Life and Death Debate*. Westport: Greenwood Press, 1990.

Moskop, J. and H. Tristram Engelhardt. "The Ethics of Suicide: A Secular View." In *Suicide: Theory and Clinical Aspects*, ed. L.D. Hankoff and B. Einsidler, 49-57. Littleton: PSG Publishing Co., Inc., 1979.

Motto, Jerome A. "The Right to Suicide: A Psychiatrist's View." In *Suicide: The Philosophical Issues*, ed. M.P. Battin and D.J. Mayo, 212-219. London: Peter Owen, 1990.

Murphy, George. "Suicide and the Right to Die." *American Journal of Psychiatry* 130 (April 1973): 472-72.

Nagel, Thomas. "The Absurd." *The Journal of Philosophy* 68 (1971): 716-27.

Nietzsche, Friedrich. *The Portable Nietzsche*. Translated and edited by Walter Kaufmann. New York: Viking, 1954.

Novak, David. *Suicide and Morality*. New York: Scholars Studies Press, 1975.

O'Keeffe, Terence M. "Suicide and Self-Starvation." In *Suicide: Right or Wrong?*, ed. John Donnelly, 117-34. Buffalo: Prometheus Books, 1990.

Plato. *Phaedo*. In *The Last Days of Socrates*, trans. Hugh Tredennick. Middlesex: Penguin, 1954.

------. *Laws*. Translated by R.G. Bury. Cambridge: Harvard University Press, 1967.

Rauscher, William V. *The Case Against Suicide*. New York: St. Martin's, 1981.

Ringel, Erwin. "Suicide Prevention and the Value of Human Life." In *Suicide: The Philosophical Issues*, ed. M.P. Battin and D.J. Mayo, 205-211. London: Peter Owen, 1980.

Ross, David. *Kant's Ethical Theory*. Oxford: Oxford University Press, 1969.

Schopenhauer, Arthur. *On the Basis of Morality*. Translated by E.F.J. Payne. Indianapolis: Bobbs-Merrill, 1965.

------. *The World as Will and Representation*. Translated by E.F.J. Payne. Vol. 1. New York: Dover Publications, Inc., 1969.

------. "On Suicide." In *Parerga and Paralipomena*. Translated by E.F.J. Payne. Vol. 2. Oxford: Oxford University Press, 1974.

Seneca. "The Stoic View." In *Suicide: Right or Wrong?*, ed. John Donnelly, 27-32. Buffalo: Prometheus Books, 1990.

Shirer, William. *The Rise and Fall of the Third Reich*. New York: Simon and Schuster, 1960.

Shneidman, Edwin S. "Preventing Suicide." In *Suicide: Right or Wrong?*, ed. John Donnelly, 153-64. Buffalo: Prometheus Books, 1990.

Singer, Peter. "Unsanctifying Human Life." In *Ethical Issues Relating to Life and Death*, ed. John Ladd. Oxford: Oxford University Press, 1979.

Slater, Eliot. "Choosing the Time to Die." In *Suicide: The Philosophical Issues*, ed. M.P. Battin and D.J. Mayo, 199-204. London: Peter Owen, 1980.

Smith, Michael. "Did Socrates Kill Himself Intentionally?" *Philosophy* 55 (1980): 253-54.

Stern-Gillet, Suzanne. "The Rhetoric of Suicide." In *Suicide: Right or Wrong?*, ed. John Donnelly, 93-103. Buffalo: Prometheus, 1990.

Sullivan, Roger. *Immanuel Kant's Moral Theory*. Cambridge: Cambridge University Press, 1989.

Szasz, Thomas S. "The Ethics of Suicide." In *Suicide: The Philosophical Issues*, ed. M.P. Battin and D.J. Mayo, 185-198. London: Peter Owen, 1980.

Tolhurst, William E. "Suicide, Self-Sacrifice, and Coercion." In *Suicide: Right or Wrong?*, ed. John Donnelly, 77-92. Buffalo: Prometheus Books, 1990.

Wheeler, Arthur M. "Suicide Intervention and False Desires." *Journal of Value Inquiry* 20 (1986): 241-244.

Williams, Glanville. *The Sanctity of Life and the Criminal Law*. New York: Alfred A. Knopf, 1974.

Windt, Peter Y. "The Concept of Suicide." In *Suicide: The Philosophical Issues*, ed. M.P. Battin and D.J. Mayo, 39-47. London: Peter Owen, 1980.

Wolman, Benjamin B., ed. *International Encyclopedia of Psychiatry, Psychology, Psychoanalysis, and Neurology*. New York: Aesculapius Publishers, Inc., 1977. S.v. "Suicidal Patients: Hospital Treatment," by Alan A Stone.

Wood, David. "Suicide as Instrument and Expression." In *Suicide: The Philosophical Issues*, ed. M.P. Battin and D.J. Mayo, 151-160. London: Peter Owen, 1980.

Wreen, Michael. "The Definition of Suicide." *Social Theory and Practice* 14 (Spring 1988): 1-23.

Young, Robert. "What Is So Wrong with Killing People?" *Philosophy* 54 (1979): 515-28.

INDEX

For Product Safety Concerns and Information please contact our EU
representative GPSR@taylorandfrancis.com
Taylor & Francis Verlag GmbH, Kaufingerstraße 24, 80331 München, Germany

www.ingramcontent.com/pod-product-compliance
Lightning Source LLC
Chambersburg PA
CBHW050714280326
41926CB00088B/3023